Liberando

Reflections of a Reluctant Warrior

John E. Horn

HOOSICK FALLS, NEW YORK
2017

First published in 2017 by the Merriam Press

First Edition

Copyright © 2017 by John E. Horn
Book design by Ray Merriam
Additional material copyright of named contributors.

ISBN 9781576385623
Library of Congress Control Number: 2016918768
Merriam Press #WM15-P

This work was designed, produced, and published in
the United States of America by the

Merriam Press
133 Elm Street Suite 3R
Bennington VT 05201

E-mail: ray@merriam-press.com
Web site: merriam-press.com

The Merriam Press publishes new manuscripts on historical subjects, especially military history and with an emphasis on World War II, as well as reprinting previously published works, including reports, documents, manuals, articles and other materials on historical topics.

Dedication

For my Dad and those of the greatest generation who, as Lincoln described, gave their last full measure.

Bronze monument in the Sicily–Rome American Cemetery and Memorial in Nettuno, Italy, where more than 7,861 American war dead, killed in the Italian Campaign, are interred.
Author's photograph.

Rear Cover

The top image is a sideview painting of a Consolidated B-24H Liberator of the 376th Bomb Group.

Osprey via author, used with permission

The other image is of a page from John H. Horn's log book.

Via author

Contents

Chapter 1

Foreword

WRITING Liberando was a labor of love and respect for my dad and an attempt to provide an understanding to his family, now and in the future, of what Dad's part was in keeping the world safe for them. Writing his war story was an incredible learning experience about memory, research, documentation, and, frankly, the amount of information available to anyone with a modicum of interest in their family's military experiences.

The primary source documents for the book were memories of Dad's childhood, communicated to me by him and family members; an interview with Dad conducted in 1999; letters from my father to his mother (Grandma Horn) during his initial entry and training in the Army Air Force; and official records from his training. Unfortunately, Grandma Horn's letters to him were not preserved and I could only speculate on what they might have said.

For the time of Dad's overseas service, four primary source documents were used:

- A hand-typed mission summary compiled by Harvey Ulmer, his flight engineer, which contained the date, mission number (by Harvey's count), mission location, a brief summary of what transpired on the mission, the aircraft number, and the time flown. Harvey was a check engineer who flew missions with other crews to qualify new engineers in the unit. Although unstated, I suspect that his summaries included some of these other missions.
- A brief mission list compiled by Dad that contained the date, mission number (by his count), mission destination, and flight time logged.

- Dad's original flight logbook, which recorded the date, aircraft type, mission destination, and time flown. Logbooks are held in such esteem that they are considered a legal document.
- A massive tome, the 376th Bomb Group Mission History, which is an extraction of the official Army Air Force records maintained in the U.S. Air Force, Air War College Library, at Maxwell Air Force Base, Alabama. It was authored by Edward F. McClendin, Jr., the son of a pilot in the 376th Bomb Group during Dad's tenure.

Finally, the author conducted two interviews with residents of San Pancrazio in 2015 which are included in the appendices.

It quickly became evident that these primary documents were frequently in disagreement, even on the most important aspect of a combat mission: the mission destination on a given date. The two most authoritative sources, Dad's logbook and the *Mission History*, were no exceptions to the incongruity among sources.

Where the primary sources disagreed, I deferred to the *376th Bomb Group Mission History* simply for consistency. However, having personally experienced official record keeping in the crucible of combat, I have no illusions concerning its absolute accuracy.

Numerous secondary sources were also employed: books, interviews, and personal and family recollections, all of which are listed in the Works Consulted section of this book. All the documentation was preserved in my personal archive and is available for those with further interest.

I tried to weave a narrative based on these source documents that is technically and historically accurate. All the events happened, but they might not have happened in the order described or to the person to whom they have been ascribed. Such is the nature of reconstructing history. All quotations in the book are the words of my dad, unless otherwise noted.

The title of the book, *Liberando: Reflections of a Reluctant Warrior*, was decided upon after much thought and input from my siblings. The "Liberandos" was the nickname of the 376th Heavy Bombardment Group of which dad was a member; ergo, the singular Liberando. The second part of the title portrays my father's essentially peaceable temperament and attitude toward the war. It wasn't in his nature to be a warrior, but it was his duty.

General George S. Patton famously said, "Duty is the essence of manhood." By all measures, then, Dad was tested and measured up. He was not a gung-ho crusader: just the opposite. He accepted his responsibility and did the best job he could for his country and family, and it was a heroic job.

He did not enjoy doing what the war required of him and he was always reluctant to discuss his wartime experiences. The few times he talked to me about it, I came away with the impression that while he was overseas, he lived in a permanent state of hypervigilance and fear. In this, he was no different from the other pilots.

My own air combat experience taught me that anyone who says he was not afraid is disingenuous. Dad's ability to control his fear, maintain vigilance, and inspire confidence by keeping his own counsel in these, plus his technical competence, was what made him a successful combat leader. There is no question he felt an absolute responsibility and concern for his crew. The sad loss of SSG Allen Bunker, his sense of letting his crew down over the forced landing at Nettuno, and the way he communicated with his crew demonstrated this. I would summarize Dad's leadership traits as character, concern, and competence. For those of you who choose to lead, these are worthy of emulation.

My own literary limitations guarantee that there are errors in the text. I retain sole responsibility for them. Even a short work like this puts the author in the debt of others who helped to make it happen. First, thank you to my brothers and sisters, Kathy, Chris, Dennis, and Rosemary, for their recollections included herein and their interest and encouragement. My sincere appreciation to my daughter, Lisa, for her editing skills earned as a newspaper woman. Also thanks to my friend in history, Orfilio Pelaez, for his help in editing. This book would not have been possible without the professional editing of my friend and colleague, Linda Manley. Finally, my heartfelt appreciation and love to my wife, Betty, for her forbearance, feedback, editing, and total support in the writing of Liberando.

John E. Horn
October 2015

Terms and Abbreviations

Ace .... A pilot who shot down five or more enemy aircraft.

A/D .... Aerodrome, airport.

Ash-and-trash .... An administrative mission that facilitated either distribution or collection of mail, men, or supplies and was flown entirely over friendly territory.

APU .... Auxiliary power unit, a small engine that powered a generator and supplied power to the B-24 when the engines were not running.

Buy the farm .... Crash; crash land; get shot down.

Deuce and a half .... The standard Army 2½-ton truck, sometimes referred to as a six by six, because all six wheels could be engaged to drive it.

DI .... A drill instructor, usually a non-commissioned officer placed in charge of military trainees. Such men were so thoroughly trained in pain and suffering that they could give the Marquis de Sade pointers.

Feet wet .... Flying over water.

Flak .... Flak was originally a German acronym for Fliegerabwehrkanonen, from flieger (flyer) + abwehr (defense) + kanonen (cannons), which basically means antiaircraft gun. Flak also referred to antiaircraft artillery and the bursting shells from such artillery.

Flat hat or flat hatting .... Low-level flying.

FNG .... F...ing (F-word) new guy.

FPM .... Feet per minute, a measurement of the rate of climb.

Greenhouse .... The cockpit of a B-24, so named because it consisted of multiple glass panels surrounding the pilot's station to allow maximum visibility.

Intel .... Intelligence.

IP .... Initial point, a geographic point on the ground where the bomb run began and the bombardier took control of the aircraft.

KIA .... Killed in action.

Patch of the 376th Heavy Bombardment Group.
376th Heavy Bombardment Group, Inc., via author.

Liberandos .... The official nickname of the 376th Heavy Bomb Group. The nickname was a variation of the name given to the B-24, the Liberator. The Liberandos emblem was a blue shield bordered by yellow, in base, a stylized winged sphinx yellow, shaded orange, edged blue, resting on a terra cotta red base. In the upper right is a yellow bomb, pointing downward, with a blue disc and triangle and a terra cotta red diamond and square. The blue and yellow are the colors of the Air Force. The winged sphinx in yellow is symbolic of the service in the Middle East Theater, where the Group began its first historical tradition. The diamond, circle, square, and triangle are for each squadron's service in Palestine. The blue of the field is also emblematic of the intense blue of the African sky at night and represents the theater where the group's missions were successfully accomplished. The terra cotta red beneath the winged sphinx is symbolic of the desert around Gambut, Soluch, and Benghazi, Libya. Liberandos is a romantic coining from the B-24 Liberator. The bomb in the right side of the shield is emblematic of the missions of the 376th Bombardment Group. (376th Heavy Bombardment Group, 2013)

MIA...............................Missing in action.

MAP..............................Manifold pressure, which is a measurement of an aircraft engine's power expressed in inches of mercury (in/Hg).

Milk run........................A routine combat mission in which nothing unexpected or hazardous occurred.

Propeller feathering........A procedure used when an engine has to be shut down in flight to twist the propeller blades so they are aligned with the aircraft direction. This prevents them from "wind-milling" and causing additional drag.

OD .... Olive drab was the color that most everything in the Army was painted.

Ops .... Refers to the section in the 376th that was responsible for all aircraft operations. The ops officer was the third ranking member of the unit and was frequently the flight leader on combat missions. The ops office was the operational heart of unit where all mission briefings took place.

Pathfinder .... Specialty radar-equipped bombers that allowed bombing with no visibility of the target. These were particularly useful when the Germans tried to obscure the targets with smoke.

Pickle button .... The trigger to fire weapons or drop bombs.

POL .... Petroleum, oil, and lubricant, used to refer to all petroleum products.

Recce............................ Reconnaissance.

R&R .... Rest and recuperation.

San Pan .... San Pancrazio, Italy, where the 376th Heavy Bomb Group was stationed.

SOP.............................. Standard operating procedures.

SS .... Schutzstaffel, literally "defense squadron." The SS was an internal security force of Nazi Germany, consisting of police and military organizations.

Standard day .... For pilots, a measurement of barometric pressure: 29.92 in/Hg and temperature of 59°F (15°C) at sea level. These measurements were used to calculate aircraft performance.

Time .... All time used in this book was military and was based on the 24-hour clock.

Flight time was expressed similarly, using four digits and a plus sign, as is the custom in military flying. Thus, 07+45 means seven hours and forty-five minutes. Flight time was always rounded to the nearest five minutes.

Temperature lapse rate ... The standard temperature lapse rate is one in which the temperature decreases at the rate of approximately 3.5°F or 2°C per thousand feet increase in altitude, up to 36,000 feet, which is approximately -65°F or -55°C. Above this point, the temperature is considered constant up to 80,000 feet.

WIA .... Wounded in action.

Chapter 1

How Am I Going to Get Out of This?

ON May 24, 1944, I was sitting in the greenhouse in one of more than 600 B-24s flying formation at 20,000 feet, headed toward the German fighter factory at Weiner-Neustadt, Austria. We had just passed the IP (initial point) on the bomb run and the bombardier had control of the ship approaching the airfield target. I had a moment to allow thoughts, other than terror, to creep into my consciousness.

The sky was crystal clear except for the hundreds of innocuous looking, but lethal black, white, and sometimes red puffs all around us. The colors indicated the caliber of the weapons: black were 88 mm shells, white were 120 mm shells, and red were smaller caliber anti-aircraft shells seen only at altitudes below 15,000 feet.

This intense and accurate fire was creating havoc in the formation. I mean, you couldn't help flinching when a shell exploded so close that the entire airplane shuddered from the shock or when you heard metal ripping. When the pilot flinched on the controls, aircraft within the formation could move in unexpected ways, causing a ripple effect.

Occasionally this resulted in mid-air collisions, which were always fatal and were the danger I feared most. More often, flinching resulted in fright, evasive action, and sometimes fouled underwear. Formation flying was one of the most hazardous, and to me, the scariest part of piloting a B-24.

Prior to reaching the target area, the formation had been attacked by multiple Me 109s from above and behind. This was the usual tactic of Luftwaffe fighters. They dove toward the formation and split into groups of three, attacking from different directions. The enemy fighters were swarming all around us prior to the target area. This unsettled the formation and caused it to spread out. Our fighter escort kept most of them at bay, but we knew they would be waiting outside the target area for the flak to do its job and would attack again on our withdrawal.

On the way to the target, and despite our fighter cover, a suicidal Luftwaffe pilot in a Me 109 screamed through the formation so close, "I could see his face." His 20-millimeter cannon sprayed fire through the formation. Several ships took hits and 2nd Lieut. Rob Matthews, flying Lonesome Polecat in the First Flight, went down. With all this going on, 2nd Lieut. J.P. Graham, flying the ship immediately to our front and above, was getting antsy because he started easing down on top of us; I'm thinking, "Oh sh.., here we go!" We were required to maintain radio silence on missions, but I broke the silence, without identifying myself to avoid repercussions later, and barked, "Graham, steady up, you are settling." Thankfully, he got the message and tightened up.

At face value, the enemy fighter tactic of a high-speed, head-on approach through a bomber formation seemed suicidal, but in reality, it was an economy of force tactic. First, the enemy approached the front of the formation where the massed defensive guns of the bombers were the weakest and his cross section was the smallest. Second, the rate of closure between the fighter and the formation was the sum of the two speeds, usually 400-600 miles per hour, thus minimizing his exposure to the formation's guns. Third, the high-speed pass impacted the greatest number of bombers, creating havoc within the formation and resulting in flinching, immediate evasive action, a separated formation, and occasionally mid-air collisions, all of which rendered the bomber formation combat-ineffective until they could regroup.

When this tactic was employed near the IP, the bombing was usually ineffective because the formation could not regroup and stabilize before the planes reached the target. The downside for the enemy pilot was that he might get caught up in the havoc among the bombers. This was a major downside, because although the Germans were actually able to increase fighter production until VE day, despite allied attempts to curtail it, Germany simply ran out of experienced pilots and could not replace them, as Capps reported in his 2004 narrative.

In the midst of this circus of terror over Weiner-Neustadt, all I could think of was, "How did I get here and how am I going to get out of this?" This was a recurring reflection and nightmare during my time overseas. To this day, I still wonder how we made it. "I never thought I would get home." My mother's daily Masses and Divine Providence were the only plausible explanation.

This was our 6th/7th mission since arriving in Italy and was by far the worst. It counted as two missions because of the danger. The first few missions were milk runs, designed for us to gain experience and build confidence. The technique worked in general, although I felt a deficit of both the entire time I was overseas. After the first few missions, some of the guys had acquired a bit of the swagger and bravado typical of young guys who had not yet come face to face with the reality of air combat: the fact that he/we were not invincible and we could actually die here.

That all changed after this mission. Our group was lucky and lost only one bomber. Our ship had 30 holes and rips in it and the others in the group were similarly damaged. Many had dead and or wounded crewmen.

From that point forward, any notion of bravado was patently ridiculous for all but the insane. And there were a few of those among us. Nick Kowalski was a pilot of Polish descent from Pittsburgh. He never lost his bravado. He was occasionally a liability because of his erratic behavior, but he was courageous and never turned back for a minor squawk. You had to like the guy, but also had to be wary of what he might do. He was also the best poker player in the squadron, frequently doubling his Army pay with his winnings.

After mission 6/7, my attitude privately was a dread of what was to come next. Outwardly my approach was sort of "work-a-day"; that is, we had a job to do, let's get it done as safely as possible. It was a young leader's attempt to inspire confidence, which in my own heart I lacked.

Initially, I thought the whole war and my small part of it was to be more of an endurance contest: separation from my family, long hours, bad food, rough living conditions, and such. Everything I had experienced in the service so far—applying to the aviation cadet program; training all over the country in Nashville, Alabama, Arkansas, Illinois, and Boise; aiming the B-24 for 11 hours across the ocean toward Africa (and actually finding it!); and now looking at flying 50 missions—all indicated tenacity was going to be the key strength required for a successful conclusion. To say that this was uninformed is an understatement.

As a 23-year-old, I was the oldest in my crew, but I wasn't exactly seasoned. The youngest was Ed Seibert, the tail gunner, who celebrated his 18th birthday while we were training at Gowen Field, Idaho. Somewhere in between was typical. We were woefully underprepared for what we faced. The definition of a successful conclusion of the war for our country was pretty clear: total defeat of the Axis.

For me, a successful conclusion was a moving target. It started out to be coming home to my new wife, Eleanore, Mom and Pop, and the rest of the family, looking appropriately dashing in my decorated uniform and bearing exotic gifts from Europe. That all changed with mission 6/7, which intimidated us so completely. Subsequently, my definition of success became to simply get us home alive with all faculties and limbs. As time went on, I just wanted to get us home alive without qualification!

After Weiner-Neustadt, my enthusiasm for risk evaporated. It dawned on me that war was neither a grand adventure nor an endurance test. To survive and do my job as the aircraft commander, the most important thing to learn was the ability to control my own fear.

Second most important was, if not to inspire confidence, then to communicate to my crew that they were a priority, and job number one was to get them home. I did this primarily by making sure everyone understood that we were completely interdependent in success or failure, that they were valued and trusted, and that we would solve problems as a team. I ensured that everyone on the crew understood their job and did it.

We shared whatever good things I could accrue—whether cookies from mom, better booze from the officer's club, cigarette rations, or time off—equally among the crew. Those were the things I could control. The rest of the affair—Germans, other airplanes in our formation, and missions were beyond my control. It goes without saying that after mission 6/7, I took no more risk than the brass forced on us, and "My dependence on the Lord rose to new highs during the war."

In 1944 the tactics, logistics, and, frankly, the casualty rates dictated that bomber crews fly 50 missions overseas before returning to the states. Earlier in the war, crews in the 8th Air Force flying out of England flew only 25-35 missions because of even higher casualty rates, which simply were not sustainable. Thank God, I didn't get to the war any earlier. Even so, an infantryman had a better chance of survival than a bomber crewman had, a fact that was conveniently omitted during my recruitment and training. I wouldn't have listened anyway.

I was jolted back into reality as the airplane lurched vertically when the bombs were loosed on the target. The voice of the bombardier, Charlie Freeman, came through the intercom, "Take us home, Cap." I was a second lieutenant at the time, but the pilot and aircraft commander was always referred to as Cap, Captain, or Skipper. I disengaged the bombsight autopilot and took control of the airplane. I felt better already: no more dreaming and something to concentrate on. I reminded everyone to keep their heads on a swivel, looking for the inevitable German fighters waiting just outside flak range and flinching aircraft within the formation.

Once in a formation, where our airplane actually went had very little to do with me. We were entirely dependent on the formation leader, because we were just one of 37 airplanes in our group formation, one of 160 bombers in our Wing (the 47th Bomb Wing), and on this day, one of 600 B-24s on the raid from the 15th Air Force. The lead bomber's navigator was in charge of where we went and how we got there.

I had the best navigator in the squadron, Frank Belasco. He always knew where we were and he knew the fastest, safest way home. His navigating was occasionally at odds with the flight leader's navigator. Like most of the stuff in the service, it wasn't always the best that rose to the top. We had a saying, "Foul up and move up," which the flight leader's navigator typified. It took a lot of self-control to not follow Frank, even though we knew that was where we should be going.

On a few occasions, I tried to prompt the flight lead, usually a major (Maj.) or lieutenant colonel (Lt.-Col.) that they were off course. My promptings usually ended in a stereotypical case of the messenger getting shot, for which I found little enthusiasm. Military tradition dictated that a FNG 2nd Lieut. could not be better informed than the flight lead. Impossible!

The navigators were more pragmatic than their bosses were. They recognized their limitations and were happy to listen when off course. Frank worked out a deal with the lead navigators to send them prompts via a code. This allowed the lead navigators to save face, enabled the formation to get home by the safest and quickest route, and avoided the whole messenger-shooting thing. Eventually the squadron commander and other flight leaders caught on and impressed Frank to serve as the lead navigator on really tricky missions.

One of the crazy things about the service, especially during wartime, is that people—soldiers, air crews, sailors, all of us—become commoditized. A navigator is a navigator. They're all the same. So at least initially, assignments are a crap shoot and are based on rank, not merit. The best doesn't always end up leading.

Besides being a cracker jack navigator, Frank was my best friend. I always felt a sense of loss and insecurity when he flew with the flight leader. Of course, when he was in the lead, we did not have to worry about unnecessary detours, either.

As the formation turned south we could see Vienna, about 30 miles in the distance, a place I wanted to visit, but not this day. It was the second most heavily defended target in Europe. The flak abated as we left the target area, but the German fighters were being reinforced, probably from Graz, a place we definitely didn't want to overfly on the way out to the Adriatic.

Many of our bombers had been damaged and a malodorous mixture of gas, oil, hydraulic fluids, and smoke wafted through the formation. I asked Harvey Ulmer, the flight engineer, to survey the crew to determine the damage to our plane. Waist gunners, looking out of the B-24s from their open windows in the rear, and other gunners were valuable visual aids to the crew because they could see oil and gasoline leaks, loose cowling, and many other discrepancies that we in the cockpit could not see. They were able to detect dangerous conditions for which there may be emergency procedures to implement to keep the airplane flying. Without their eyes, I was literally flying blind.

Presently, the different voices of the nine crew members reported over the intercom from their stations; the worst problem seemed to be a sheet metal tears and damage to the fabric-covered rudders on both sides, but nothing more. On the ground, we later discovered 30 holes and rips in our ship, many of them in the fabric-covered control surfaces, the rudders, and the horizontal stabilizer. Some ships in the formation were not as lucky. I could see elevator and aileron control surfaces that were shredded. I saw large tears in the fuselage sheet metal of several planes, engines out, propellers feathered, fuel and oil leaks, and on and on.

More casualties were inevitable because of the aforementioned hemorrhage of vital fluids. The hope was that the plane was well out of enemy fighter range, in our case, over the Adriatic, before any other malfunction occurred. A lost engine meant reduced speed, and flying at reduced speed meant dropping out of the formation. Dropping out and falling behind meant the airplane was a sitting duck for attacking fighters; hence, the counter-intuitive hope of being over water, beyond enemy fighter range, when an engine or engines quit.

In addition to aircraft damage that day, we learned multiple crew members had been wounded by shrapnel as we listened to the damage reports being relayed to the flight leader. Aircraft with wounded were always given priority to land so the injured could receive prompt medical attention.

We were firing on all cylinders and I silently thanked God for that. Presently, I heard Frank sending code to the lead navigator, ensuring that we gave the fighter base in Graz a wide berth by turning southeast. Shortly thereafter, the formation began a lumbering right turn to a more southerly direction. The attacking fighters trailed off 60 miles south of Weiner-Neustadt; good news!

The next pressure relief point was the coast of Yugoslavia, where we would go feet wet over the Adriatic and be relatively safe from attacking fighters, but not from the hazards of ditching in the sea. After that, we had another four hours of flying to reach our San Pancrazio (San Pan) base. Suddenly I heard a warning of "Fighters, 12 o'clock high!" All eyes began scanning to skies to the front where I immediately saw several Me 109s.

Something was different, because they were not diving toward us. We had a fighter escort of P-47s and they had the discipline to stay with us instead of peeling off and giving chase to the enemy fighters. That was a favorite trick of the Germans: to dangle some fighters, well away from the formation, as bait for the testosterone hyper-endowed fighter pilots. When the fighter escort gave chase, another group of enemy fighters would attack the bomber formation from another direction, usually from our 6 o'clock low.

Today, the enemy had a new threat for us. The high fighters dropped aerial bombs into the formation. The bombs were fused to explode at the altitude where we were flying. We had not seen this before and it took the escort fighters a few minutes to figure out that they needed to engage the bombing enemy fighters. The aerial bombs were ineffective, but I couldn't help thinking of the irony of the whole incident: a bomber formation being bombed!

We went feet wet around 10:30 in the morning. A quick tally among the 376th Group formation netted one ship lost, three badly damaged and unable to keep up with the formation, and 12 others with damage, including #29, our ship. We landed at San Pan Airfield on a crystal clear day at 13:30, logging 08 + 00 hours.

No sooner had I cut the engines than the ground crew began swarming all over the airplane to assess what we had done to their baby. The crew chief was in charge of the airplane on the ground. A good crew chief took extreme ownership of his airplane and allowed us only to borrow it for prosecution of the war. Staff Sgt. Kirk was in the cockpit before I was unbelted, wanting to know of any issues.

About 10 hours into the day, my patience was running a bit thin and I was trying to control my trembling, caused by the utter relief at being on the ground safely. It is impossible to explain the ineffable feeling we had returning safely from a mission. In the air, the only future was the next checkpoint or procedure. Once on the ground, we could think about real life again.

I wanted to get to the intel debrief where I knew my two ounces of whiskey, presumably to calm our nerves, was waiting. But I also wanted #29 to be in top shape for the next flight, so I patiently dealt with the crew chief until all his post-flight questions were answered. Finally, Staff Sgt. Kirk helped me out of my seat and gear and I got a ride in the back of a deuce and a half to intel and that badly needed two ounces of whiskey.

The ground crews were permanently assigned to specific airplanes: they owned them. Some flight crews had assigned aircraft, but flew whatever aircraft was assigned on mission days. We left "our" airplane in Brazil before crossing because of a maintenance problem and were assigned another to ferry across the Atlantic. Because of this, my crew didn't feel particular ownership for any of the airplanes, but we knew who the best crew chiefs were and always tried to wrangle our way into their airplanes. Ground crews had a great deal of pride of ownership in their ships.

A word about the ground crews and the aircraft maintenance squadron in the 376th is in order at this point. The maintenance officer was Captain (Capt.) Gary Brower, and his sole job in life was to generate operational B-24s for the next day's mission. To accomplish this, he had a Line Chief, Master Sergeant (Master Sgt.) Blazer, the senior enlisted man in the maintenance squadron. This guy was second only to the First Sergeant of the squadron in rank, prestige, and respect. He had three Tech Sergeants

(Tech. Sgt.) flight chiefs under him, who supervised the Staff Sgt. crew chiefs assigned to each B-24.

The crew chief led three mechanics in working on their assigned airplane. Given that the 376th had 40 airplanes, plus or minus, at any given time, one can quickly calculate that there were more than 160 men working directly on the aircraft, plus all the overhead, aviation supply personnel, inspectors, and others. More than 200 men were hands-on in the effort to maintain the B-24s in a heavy bomber group. Gary Brower was a bit of a character: painfully thin, chain smoking, and constantly in need of sleep. He had the best aircraft availability rate in the group and had the best access to a supply system that could never quite catch up. He was constantly seen driving the flight line in an orange jeep, reputed to be stolen, checking on his maintenance teams.

George McGovern of presidential candidate fame said in Stephen Ambrose's Wild Blue (2002), "I was never out on the flight line at any hour of the day or night that the mechanics were not out there working. They were the most dedicated people I ever saw." Our ground crews were the most resourceful people in the unit. They always had the best of everything. If they couldn't make it, they traded for it. If they couldn't trade, they did a "five-finger requisition." Whether it was warmer clothes, steaks, beer, or anything else we needed, they had it or could get it.

We discovered one surprising example of their resourcefulness at 20,000 feet, coming home from a mission to Ploesti one day. Harvey Ulmer was doing a damage check over the Adriatic when he called me on the intercom and told me he had discovered a sheet metal compartment above the oxygen bottles, "Hey, Cap, that ain't supposed to be there and it is dripping."

I told him to check it out, and when he finally opened it (it had been riveted for security), he discovered it contained nearly a case of beer. Sadly, a few bottles immediately adjacent to several holes in the aircraft skin had become casualties. As it turned out, the crew chief liked cold beer and we had no refrigeration at San Pan. He and his mechanics built a cooler, attached it to their B-24, and loaded it with beer before each mission. When the airplane returned from several hours at high altitude, their beer was cold! Pride in their airplanes was not the only reason the crew chiefs were anxious for us to return!

B-24J undergoing field maintenance in Italy.
USAF via author.

Chapter 2

Getting to Europe

I got back from the Weiner-Neustadt mission debriefing with time for a short nap before supper. The two ounces of whiskey was wafting over me as I laid on my cot to wait for chow. Not that it was worth waiting for, as it promised to be another iteration of mystery meat, overcooked vegetables, and fruit salad, all canned. I thought canned vegetables were already cooked, but apparently, Cookie never got the word.

The best part of the meal was the crusty Italian bread. Our mess sergeant, Cookie, bought it from the local bakers to provide a welcome side to his meals. The bread was the only thing on the plate that stood out from what could charitably be described as gray-green mush. It was the only thing we ate that was fresh, save for a bit of fruit we got from the locals. One of the things I missed most about the service was Mom's cooking. "Makes my mouth water just to think about those pies" she made.

In all fairness to the Army's culinary corps, the sanitary conditions in Italy at this time were abominable. Cookie's first priority was to prevent us from dying of food poisoning, hence the sterilized, canned, and dehydrated food, so we could have the opportunity to die prosecuting the war!

Vacantly gazing up at the OD tent roof from my cot, my mind wandered to the persistent question, which again presented itself over the target today. If not particularly profound, the question was ever-present and it nagged me, "How did I end up in this?"

The first time I remember any interest in flying was when Charles Lindbergh made his solo non-stop flight across the Atlantic Ocean. I was 6 years old in May 1927 when the country went crazy over this singular accomplishment. It was huge, front-page news for days, the biggest thing in the country. People who had no interest in aviation, including Mom and Pop, became fascinated and immediate enthusiasts. That it kindled a lifelong interest in this first-grader was evidence of the significance of the event.

Where we lived in Poughkeepsie, New York was not exactly aviation central, and an airplane flying overhead was an event. Mom and Pop said once I discovered Lindbergh, my course for life was set toward an aviation career. Knowing what I wanted to do was one of the great gifts in my life. From that point on, when an airplane flew overhead, I looked up.

Between toys, model airplanes, magazines, stories on the radio, and the occasional sighting, I couldn't get enough. The military value of the airplane had been proven in World War I and Lindbergh's solo transatlantic crossing proved its potential worth for commercial travel. It had the effect of bringing the technology from the realm of Flash Gordon into everyday life.

The depression arrived with the stock market crash of 1929 in New York. Pop lost his job selling provisions to restaurants and hotels in 1930. The Crash put most of his customers out of business almost overnight. Pop was originally from Joplin, Missouri, and had family and connections in the Midwest. The depression had not hit the Midwest yet and Mom and Pop thought it might be a better place to ride it out. They decided to make the move.

In 1930, all of us—my two sisters, Marguerite (Maggie) and Harriet, and my brother, Ed, Mom and Pop, and I—piled into the ancient Studebaker and headed west. We had been on the road four days when we pulled into Baxter Springs, Kansas. I have three memories of the trip: the incessant game I invented for us kids to see who could look out the car windows and find the most airplanes; my mother's waning patience, which was directly proportional to our westerly progress; and the brand new brick house we drove up to in Baxter Springs. Pop had the money for a down payment, got a mortgage, and purchased the house sight unseen. It was small, but pretty spectacular compared to the frame houses that were fixtures in Poughkeepsie. Only the wealthy had brick houses there. Presently, we were enrolled in school and we settled into a routine.

One of the advantages of Kansas, for me, was that it was home to several aviation manufacturers: Cessna, Stearman, Beechcraft, and Travelaire. There was a lot more aviation activity in Kansas, which fed my obsession with all things flying. It was commonplace to see airplanes overhead, so much so that it was difficult to keep my mind on my fourth-grade studies, a pattern that continued throughout my school days and doomed me to mediocrity as a student.

One of the highlights was the walk to and from the school building. There were a lot of undeveloped, overgrown plots of land on the route, which our juvenile curiosity called us to explore. My brother Ed and I had discovered the vertical shaft of a fallow lead mine in one field we crossed and we used to love to lay down with our heads over the edge and shout into to it, listening to the echoes, or to drop rocks and try to hear them hit bottom. It must have been pretty deep, because we hardly ever heard them hit bottom.

This activity lasted for half the school year before being discovered. I lost my jacket in the mine, carelessly allowing it too close to the edge, where somehow it was swallowed. At first Mom didn't believe the story of how I lost the jacket, but pretty quickly, her concern for the lost jacket was overcome by her concern that we had been lying over the edge of a bottomless abyss. Anyway, she put an end to our mining adventures. She told Pop and he sealed the deal with a couple of whacks from his belt.

Just as it seemed we were settling in with our routine, Mom and Pop said we were moving back to New York. They didn't say why, but I found out later that Pop couldn't get a job in Kansas and they thought there were better options in New York. A sad fact that I learned later was that Mom and Pop had to walk away from that brand new brick house, losing everything. The real estate market had dried up in Baxter Springs. Just as the Depression had begun on Wall Street and traveled westward across the country, so did the recovery begin in New York.

Travel suited me and I was all for another road trip. Off we went in the beat-up Studebaker to our new home in Newburgh, just down the road from Poughkeepsie.

We arrived in Newburgh and moved into a nice, two-story house at 235 Carpenter Avenue. Pop got a job with Canada Dry beverages and that effectively was the end of the depression for our family. It was the job he held until the war started in 1942. There was still a lot of frugality in our house, but we always had food to eat, clothes to wear, and the necessities.

We felt comparatively well off and did what we could through the church to help others. Mom became the queen of the soup kitchen at St. Mary's Church. There she saw sadness and need, which I knew she felt could be our family. Her parents, the Carneys, had emigrated from Ireland to the United States because of hunger. It was both cathartic for her and effective control for me. She could artfully weave the sadness and need she saw into a guilt trip, humble me, and make me feel worse than if I had been hided.

In 1931, my model airplane period began and I became very proficient at building and flying gliders and rubber-band-powered models. In those days, models were a bunch of balsa wood sheets and sticks and tissue paper, accompanied by a detailed set of plans. Each part of the model was transferred from the plans to the balsa and then cut with a razor blade. When the fragile balsa wood skeleton was complete, it was covered with tissue paper that was then sprayed with water so it would shrink around the frame. The final process was coating it with model airplane dope, a redolent substance that hardened the tissue paper, forming a smooth skin over which the air could flow efficiently. The whole progression was tedious, but in the end, very satisfying and instructive in manual skills.

We flew these in all sorts of contests: highest climb in flight, longest duration flight, and closed course flying, where the flyer tried to trim (adjust the control surfaces) on the model before launching so it would fly a specific course. One of the Horn family legends was the rubber-band-powered model I built named Homesick. It was trimmed to be launched from the front porch of the Carpenter Avenue house, make a complete circle around the house, and run out of power right where I launched it. Homesick was a thing of beauty and never failed to garner compliments on my airmanship. Model building increased my interest in aviation and anything that was hands-on. I took wood shop in high school and made all the usual baubles for Mom and even some worthwhile furniture, at least one piece of which still exists.

As far as travel goes, we didn't do much of it after landing back in Newburgh. Well, there was that time, as a 10 year-old, that a friend and I decided to ride our coaster scooters to Poughkeepsie to see my friend Richard Birdsall. It was a distance of some 18 miles. We crossed the bridge to Beacon, New York, and proceeded to scoot our way up Route 2. When I didn't appear for lunch, Mom began to worry, and by the time Pop got home, she was frantic.

We made it to Richard's house in six hours but missed lunch! When we arrived there, Mrs. Birdsall asked where my family was, assuming that we had traveled together. When I told her they were at home and that we had come up on our own, she went slightly hysterical and immediately called mom. That resulted in Pop showing up at the Birdsall's post haste with a not-too-happy look on his face.

I could usually count on Pop to understand, and Mom was the disciplinarian. I could tell that wasn't going to work in this instance. Mom had obviously gotten him spun up over my unauthorized absence and there were going be consequences. My solo traveling days ended in the basement in an encounter with Pop's belt.

In high school, I was 140 pounds and made it to 6 feet tall by my senior year. Participation in sports or being a fan didn't really interest me except for major league baseball. Pop rooted for the St. Louis Cardinals because of his formative years growing up in Joplin. I couldn't identify with them and selected the New York Giants to support. I was very proud when my younger brother Ed adopted the Giants too.

High school, for me, was spent trying to figure out how to become a pilot, as opposed to concentrating on my studies. Aviation in the 30s was hands-on and maintenance-intensive. Pilots were expected to be able to fix their planes themselves. I threw myself into anything mechanical or woodworking, helping others work on their cars and fixing things around the house. The latter had the ancillary benefit of endearing me to Mom and getting first dibs at whatever tantalizing dessert she had on hand. I remember her as an OK cook, but a tremendous baker and dessert-maker. I developed a taste for sugar, something we never got enough of during the Depression or the War.

In the latter 30s, I remember becoming aware of the political turmoil in Europe. This was 1938-39, my last year of high school. Our teachers at the Newburgh Free Academy were very good and took the time to orient us to the realities of the world situation. That I remember being aware is a testament to their dedication.

When I graduated in 1939, I knew that aviation was where my future lay, but I didn't have a plan. Dad got me a job working for the local Ebling beer distributor in the personage of one Hans Swartzman, a friend he had made in the food and beverage business.

In those days, most beer was delivered and sold in 15-gallon wooden kegs that, when loaded, weighed around 160 pounds. I tipped the scales at 140 pounds at the time, but by using a system of slides, ramps, hand trucks, and other gadgets, it was possible for me to handle the barrels. Hans was huge and unbelievably strong. He could manhandle the barrels without the tools. Most of the in-town deliveries at this time were still done with a horse and wagon, but Ebling had given Hans a cool 1936 Ford delivery truck. We'd go down to the riverfront and load the beer barrels off the docks, where they had previously been shipped up river from the Bronx on a Hudson River Dayline steam boat.

Hans was extremely industrious and Teutonically efficient. He never wanted to make more than one trip to the docks on a given day, which resulted in some creative overloading of the truck. We never had a mishap, unless you count the time I tried to have a go with the truck. Hans frequently lunched with our customers and I always waited in the truck during these languid repasts because Mom didn't want to hear of me hanging out in taverns.

One day, after an hour or so, I was getting antsy and hatched the idea of joy riding around the block. The truck was parked facing uphill on Broadway. The Ford started right away and I released the brake while simultaneously applying power and easing out the clutch. It stalled. Quickly applying the brakes to arrest the truck from rolling backwards downhill, I started the engine and began the process again, with the same results, and again, and again!

By my fourth try, the truck had rolled backwards 100 feet down the hill and was perilously close to a car parked behind. I was afraid to try the maneuver again and applied the parking brake, slid over to the sidewalk side of the cab and climbed down from the Ford, wondering how the movement of the truck was to be explained.

I needn't have worried because Hans and his customer were on the sidewalk laughing. All the noisy engine revving brought them outside to investigate, where they enjoyed at least my last few attempts at driving. Hans said nothing, turned around, and went back in the tavern for another half hour. During the ensuing wait, I wondered what Pop would say about me losing the job he got for me. Hans finally emerged from lunch, got in, and said, "Guess we git you some truck drivin' lessons, ya?"

True to his word, he taught me to how to drive. Eventually I learned to negotiate the steepest hills in Newburgh and I also became Hans's permanent driver! I settled into an easy routine with my work, but worried that my dream of flying was not being advanced.

Having a paying job that connected me to the community and working with someone I liked and respected did have its satisfaction. It was easy and fun to get to know people in Newburgh, with its population of 6,000, essentially working on the sidewalk outside of places where folks met to socialize. In fact, that's how I met Eleanore, who, as you know, became my wife, your mother, grandmother, great grandmother, and so on. She was the second great gift in my life.

Eleanore had been a friend of Marguerite, my older sister. I had always admired her from afar, but had never gone beyond a simple hello. Hans and I were stocking the Palatine Hotel, which had a great elevator from the sidewalk into the basement where they stored their beer. I was rolling barrels off the truck onto the elevator platform when "she" walked by in what I assumed was a nurse's uniform. By this time, in 1941, I had developed an easy and familiar style with the people on our route and thought nothing of greeting whoever walked by. My charm abandoned me on this day and I was at a loss for words.

Eventually, something polite must have stuttered forth because Eleanore Hamway acknowledged me politely and walked in the front door of the hotel. I was pretty much in awe of her from that day forward. Hans told me that her dad, Ed Hamway, was the bartender in the Palatine, that Eleanore worked for a dentist, Dr. McGrath, and that sometimes she came to the hotel to have lunch with her dad. I wondered how Hans knew so much about her, and I later discovered that Eleanore's mom was of German descent; hence, the connection.

Newburgh was originally settled by Germans, then by the Scots and Irish, and now apparently by the Lebanese, because Hans told me that's where Mr. Hamway was from. The German residents considered themselves just a cut above the rest since they were the first settlers in the area, although currently, the aggressive behavior of Germany in Europe diminished their standing in the community and caused some small suspicion.

Life got more interesting for me in Newburgh from that point forward and I spent a lot of time trying to run into Eleanore. I asked her out several times but she politely declined, saying I was too young. My mother said the same thing, but I was undeterred and the rest is history.

The war in Europe was on the front page of the Newburgh News every day. The sleeping industrial giant in the United States was awakening to equip the Allied forces. Britain and

France had declared war on Germany in 1939, shortly after Hitler broke another of his treaties of convenience by invading Poland. By May 1940, Germany had pushed the British expeditionary force off the continent at Dunkirk, and France surrendered a few weeks later to be occupied and plundered for four long years. Italy and Japan formally joined Germany in the Axis Pact in September 1940.

The talk of the United States actually getting into the war was muted, but the national determination to assist those confronting the Axis powers, directly, was clear. The Germans were threatening U.S. "Lend Lease" shipping to Britain, but this wasn't yet enough to rouse the American will to fight. It would take the Japanese attack on Pearl Harbor a year later to do that.

There was no mistaking that materiel preparations for conflict were ongoing. Roosevelt signed the Selective Service Act, requiring all men between 18 and 35 to register and requiring that they serve 12 months of active service. In the spring of 1941, Roosevelt asked for and Congress approved an extension of the 12-month period of service for an indefinite period. It became clear that all able-bodied men would be going in the service as soon as the government figured out how to implement the new conscription laws.

All this was not lost on me and my aspirations to become an aviator. One of the new programs that a prescient Gen. Hap Arnold introduced to fill the ranks of desperately needed pilots for the Army Air Corps was called the Civilian Pilot Training Program (CPTP), which began humbly in 1938. The CPTP became the War Training Service (WTS), and from 1942 to 1944, served primarily as the screening program for potential pilot candidates.

The WTS and CPTP were associated with colleges and universities. Students attended classes, including aviation ground school subjects, and the flight training was conducted by private flight schools contracted by the government. All WTS/CPTS graduates were required to sign a contract agreeing to enter the military following graduation. I had never given much thought to attending college, but Pearl Harbor, the prospect of getting free flying lessons, and then flying in the Army overcame any reluctance about further schooling.

I enrolled at New Paltz State Teachers College in January of 1942, the entire object of which was to get the CPTP flight training and enroll in Aviation Cadet Training Program (AvCad) of the Army Air Corps. I had saved some money working for Hans and could just about afford a semester or two, including the ancient Model T Ford I would need to go back and forth between home and Kingston, where the college was located. It was difficult to say goodbye to Hans. Always understanding, we shared a last beer in his favorite tavern and he slipped a few extra dollars in my pay envelope.

New Paltz State was about the same size as the Newburgh Free Academy and the memories of academic drudgery were not appealing, but the lure of the CPTP made it bearable. There were two CPTP classes each semester, lasting three months. I drew the course that started in the last half of the semester, from April to June. I needed to be doing well enough academically by April to begin flying. The semester was a blur, traveling to Kingston, then to Hackensack airfield where the CPTP took place, then home and start all over again. Thanks to Hans, I could drive, and my hands-on experience kept the Model T Ford running with bailing wire, Pop's money, and good luck.

To my surprise, the first three months of the semester before flying weren't so bad. In fact, I began to enjoy academics. My favorite courses were history and the aviation ground school course. In April, my chance to fly came. I was standing tall at the New Hackensack airfield to meet my instructor, Mr. L.L. Dickenson, at 8:30 AM. After about an hour of ground discussion of the J3 Cub we would be flying, we took off. It is difficult to explain the feeling of flying: it was freedom; it was solitary.

Flying gives the sense of immense power and confidence. Flying made me feel like I could handle anything and gave me the confidence essential for my future. Flying was defining for me, and I was hooked from the moment we began the takeoff roll and I saw the world receding under us. It would be so for the rest of my life.

The method of instruction (MOI) was for Mr. Dickenson to discuss the flight maneuvers on the ground and demonstrate them in the air. Then I was to try to replicate them. This MOI was to be repeated at each phase of my flight training in the service and didn't change much in my 30 years of flying. You can see from the rating sheet that I had some aptitude. Once I had a taste of actual flying, I would have done anything to continue. Fortunately, the Germans and Japanese created the imperative where all I had to do was keep doing what I did on that first day.

On June 5, 1942, I took my private pilot check ride with Mr. George G. Young and passed. I was now fully qualified to pilot an airplane on my own and enter AvCad.

Despite the good experiences, I had no further interest in or purpose for attending college and the war wasn't going particularly well for the Allies. As soon as I completed the CPTP portion of college, I enlisted in the U.S. Army Air Force, on June 30, 1942. As badly as the military needed men for the nascent U.S. war machine, they apparently needed clerks more, because it took them until January 1943 to call me to active duty. In the interim, I went back to work for Hans, making decent money and spending it as fast as it came in.

Dating was expensive and I knew there wasn't much time to make an impression. More determined than ever, I ardently pursued Eleanore. Gradually I overcame her reluctance to date younger men. The median age for women to marry in 1940 was 21.5 years (Stritof, 2014). Eleanore was 23 in 1942 and might have been feeling her biological clock running, or as I later found out, feeling some pressure from her mom and Dr. McGrath, all of which was my good fortune.

Once she gave me a chance, we were in love. She had been invited to West Point near Newburgh, several times to attend cadet functions and liked the military pomp. She was excited about my aviation aspirations and military life. Her parents liked me and it was game on.

The only thing restraining me was Mom withholding her endorsement. There were probably several reasons for this as I reflect on it now: I was her oldest son and no one could measure up. Eleanore's mom, Mrs. Hamway, was of German descent, and currently Germans weren't very popular. And a reason a little closer to home was Mom's Irish background. The Germans had discriminated against the Irish as later immigrant arrivals in Newburgh. So between her familial and cultural bias, Mom was in no hurry to endorse the relationship and she counseled restraint.

Eleanore was sensitive to Mom's bias and my devotion to Mom. To her everlasting credit, she did everything right in trying to win Mom over. They became great friends and loved each other very much, but that is another story. Understanding how other people felt and empathizing with them was one of Eleanore's great gifts.

By the time I was called to active service and AvCad, I was so smitten that it was hard for me to leave Eleanore. But staying wasn't an option: when Uncle Sam calls, you respond. The next 10 months were an absolute blur and whirlwind of new experiences and travelling.

My first base was the Army Air Force Southeast Training Center in Nashville, Tennessee, where I arrived by train on Friday, January 8, 1943. It was my first time in the Deep South and I had no concept of what to expect there. Nashville was the base where aviation cadets were inducted into the real Army and classified as a pilot, bombardier, or navigator. Here we underwent a facsimile of basic training. There was no flying at all.

We received our uniforms and were assigned bunks in open bay barracks with 38 of our new best friends. To accomplish classification, the Army administered endless psychological, medical, and physical testing. In between, we attended lectures to orient us to the military in subjects such as military discipline, courtesy, sex hygiene, and traditions of the military.

"We have drill periods each day as well as an athletic period when we do calisthenics. No ball games." It was not physically tough, "but it is colder than hell" in Tennessee. Let me tell you, getting up in near zero-degree weather in the barracks is shocking. "When the other fellows see me go to bed in the raw, they all let out one big brrrrr."

The rules and regulations were mighty strict. Personal appearance and maintenance of our living area were major issues. If it wasn't perfect, we paid dearly in extra training, mostly pushups, which were usually administered during meal time, further reducing the brief time we had to eat. The food was good, even though we got stew, a lot of stew. [Note: Dad disliked cooked carrots, which were most likely in the stew, for the remainder of his life.]

I quickly broke the code for the discipline and hazing though. The cadre was trying to put us under some pressure and our responses were an indication of how we might handle pressure under combat conditions. So the ticket was to listen, respond positively, make corrections if you screwed up, and not let all the yelling and harassment bother you. Of course, this was the easy part. Once we got beyond this classification center, into the actual cadet program and pre-flight training, it was more difficult.

It took a few weeks at Nashville for the Army to discover the obvious, that I was an ace, waiting to fly. I was classified as a pilot and sent to Maxwell Field, Alabama, to begin the first phase of the AvCad program, pre-flight training. Pre-flight was nine weeks of premeditated torture, and if it turned us into soldiers, so much the better. We had all the general military training, physical training, marksmanship, drill, and ceremony classes that all soldiers get in basic training. Along with these universal military classes, we studied aviation-oriented classes in aircraft recognition, Morse code, formative math, and physics tailored to our future as aviation officers.

The trip to Maxwell Army Air Force Base and Montgomery was about 300 miles in a shaky bus, but we arrived unscathed on Friday, January 22, to a reception of a screaming group of DIs. Maxwell was where the Army determined if you were officer material. There was no flying, just military training.

The place was awash with calculated and seemingly pointless rules. We couldn't look anywhere but straight ahead, we had to walk at a specific pace, but no running or talking. As lower classmen, also known as zombies, we had to walk the ratline, which meant we must walk at 140 steps per minute, chest out, shoulders back, ramrod straight, and no farther than 18 inches from the wall or curb/gutter. Walking that fast was as difficult as running. Apparently zombies weren't worthy of traversing the same paths as the rest of the world.

We didn't have talking privileges yet. Geez, whatever happened to the Constitution and freedom of speech? During meals, the rules were particularly heinous: we had to sit at attention, ramrod straight. One hand was always at your side unless cutting meat or buttering bread, eyes straight ahead.

I wondered if I could take 90 days of this. When I had doubts, I just conjured up a vision of those silver aviator wings and my ticket to the sky. Any violation of the onerous regulations earned the miscreant a turn outside on the pull-up bars or on the ground doing push-ups. This resulted in a lot of indigestion and wasted food here, but they told me the local farmers bought it for their hogs. Judging from all the uneaten food, at least the local hogs were well fed. There were a lot of us who missed meals before we understood the rules. The code I learned in Nashville worked here, too: you can't let the DIs see you crack. Be professional, be responsive, and learn; behind your face, think whatever will get you through the immediate crisis.

We started our physical training immediately. In addition to calisthenics, we ran seven miles more or less on a cross-country course. A quarter of the fellows in my squadron got sick at Maxwell, including me, with a nagging sore throat and cold. The doctor told me to lay off the physical training for a few days. I wasn't unhappy about the respite! Our class really didn't get on the normal schedule until the first week in February. The running and calisthenics were the most physically challenging things I had ever done. My arms and legs felt like they would fall off. Some of the guys fainted or even cried. The DIs said it would get easier as we become conditioned. I was a little ashamed to realize how far out of shape I was. I prayed for conditioning!

As far as academics go, we took math, military courtesy and customs, physics, maps and charts, aircraft recognition, signal communications, and ground forces. These classes lasted five weeks. When I became an upperclassman in the last four weeks, there were additional classes. I hadn't had any exams yet, but I was confident that with hard work, I would do well.

Then, of course, there was the unending shoe shining, uniform maintenance, barracks cleaning, and other mundane tasks. According to the DIs, our standard of cleanliness was deplorable. If they found anything out of place during an inspection, they trashed the place and we started all over.

We got up at 0515 and the lights had to be out at 2200. There wasn't enough time in the day. I frequently had to find time for study after lights out, under my blanket with a flashlight. Of course, if you got caught studying after lights out, you could count on being up for another few hours doing calisthenics outside in the dark.

Perhaps one of the best things about being an aviation cadet was the Cadet Honor Code, which legislated that a cadet must be honest, and must not lie, cheat, or steal. Violation of the honor code was grounds for washing out, immediate dismissal from the program. That was all good.

The bad news was that if an upper classman or DI asked if you shined your shoes before each formation, which was a requirement, you had to tell the truth. And if you didn't, or failed to follow one of the other countless regulations, you received demerits. So many demerits and you had to walk a tour of duty around the squadron area with your rifle on the weekend.

It was not specifically stated, but apparently, the constitutional right to avoid self-incrimination had also been suspended in the AvCad program, along with protection against cruel and unusual punishment and freedom of speech. Compared to my upbringing and life prior to the Army, this seemed like prison. Of course, the difference was that this lasted only five weeks and then came a return to relative normalcy, and I was that much closer to flying.

About this time, I started feeling a little sorry for myself, since I hadn't received any goody packages from home recently. I really felt this when my roommate, Cadet Keith Hunt, received some great brownies and candy. That was one time I was glad that our other two roommates were sick in the hospital. Hunt and I devoured them in one day.

Readers Digest had a great article about AvCad in the February 1943 issue (Sonder, 1943). Mom and Pop read it and realized I was not exaggerating my difficulties. Guess they felt sorry for me because the goody packages became more frequent. Selfishly, I did not realize how deprived the civilian population was due to rationing of almost everything. Mom probably used the family's entire sugar ration just to keep me in goodies.

One of the activities I learned to enjoy was the parades. We marched everywhere and were well practiced in drill. Once a week, sometimes more often, we had the opportunity to compete with the other pre-flight squadrons. Parading was pure teamwork and conditioned us to respond precisely and immediately to commands. My squadron won several competitions at Maxwell. With a win came a pass (time off) from the Wing Commander, so drill and ceremony had extrinsic rewards too.

About this time, in 1943, my little brother, Ed, joined the Army. He was only 18, but he would have been drafted soon anyway. By joining, he had some options with regard to his job. Draftees were at the mercy of the "needs of the service." He had intended to follow me to the AvCad program, but the army had other needs and he ended up in the Air Defense Artillery. We were disappointed, but at least he drew one of the better ground combat jobs.

Eleanore and I had a devoted and passionate correspondence going, but it did suffer those first five weeks at Maxwell. This was the period when my mom wasn't too excited about the idea of us being serious, and it was worrisome for me, wondering how their relationship was going back in Newburgh.

As my training at Maxwell progressed, I got over my cold and sore throat and began to think the climate in the South agreed with me. We went into the altitude chamber where normally they only go up 25,000 feet, but I was doing so well they took me to 28,000 feet, where normally a person would pass out from lack of oxygen. I didn't! They checked my vital signs and then assessed my ability to understand and react. I could hear them giving me instructions, but understandably couldn't follow them very well.

My posture also started improving due to the constant haranguing of the DIs and upperclassmen. My grades were pretty decent compared to high school and the pictures I had taken in Nashville finally caught up with me. They weren't very good, but Mom, Maggie, and most importantly, Eleanore, liked them.

We were allowed off the base the last weekend in February. A few fellows and I stayed overnight Saturday in the Whitley Hotel in downtown Montgomery. It sure was nice to miss reveille. There were a couple of clubs in Montgomery run by the Army, where cadets could go to dance and have a few drinks.

By the time I became an upperclassman in March 1943, my physical conditioning had improved to the point that the day-to-day exercises and running were a breeze. I even began to gain a little weight. We were familiarized with various weapons, including the Browning automatic rifle and Thompson sub-machine gun, and we qualified with a .45 caliber pistol, which was the weapon we carried when flying missions.

Without all the harassment from the DIs and upperclassmen that I had as a zombie, the rest of the training at Maxwell seemed like a downhill ride. It was amazing how much time I had when not having to kowtow or be harassed. Of course, now it was my responsibility to mentor the zombies. Honestly, I skipped the harassment part and tried to just help them.

Just before we left Maxwell, my roommate got a letter from his brother-in-law, who was a medic during the landings in Africa. He had some horrible tales of wounded and mangled men coming through his hospital. "He says it is horrible enough to see, but to hear them all crying out for home is even worse." This was a wake-up call for me and I felt guilty complaining about my travails during training. It also clued me in to the fact that I was engaged in a deadly serious endeavor. The next part of the training, flying, would determine how I and those around me fared in combat. I made a promise to myself to redouble my efforts to become the best pilot possible.

My grades at Maxwell were surprisingly good. My previous academic career had been so unremarkable that I enjoyed sending my academic record to Mom and Dad.

The next phase of AvCad was Primary Flight Training conducted at Clarksdale, Mississippi. More men washed out of Primary than any other phase. This was where the Army found out who got airsick, who was uncoordinated, who had a fear of flying, and who had any other disqualifying condition. I approached Primary with some degree of confidence because flying was about the only Army experience I had done before. Of course, there was an Army way to fly, which surprisingly was not that much different from Mr. Dickenson's.

To say that I thrived would be an understatement. The food at Clarksdale was remarkably good. Guess it must have been a Southern thing. Clarksdale was the backwater of all backwaters and the base became an object of civic pride for the locals. Beyond red clay, agriculture, and abject poverty, there was nothing in Clarksdale. The townspeople were very supportive, often having cadets to their homes for dinner, where the food was even better than on the base.

I was invited with nine other cadets to Mr. Sam Lisenby's home for Sunday dinner. "He's a millionaire, I think, and a swell guy. We ate on beautiful china and silverware. We drank from silver goblets. It was interesting to see how the other half lives. There was a gal there, about 45 years old, that had a diamond on worth at least $5,000. The biggest thing I ever saw." [Author's note: Interesting that Dad was so observant of diamonds, even though there was no mention of engagement to Eleanore at this point.] Mr. Lisenby was really supportive of the base and did everything in the world for cadets. He even had a couple of cars just for our use.

During Primary, we flew the Boeing Stearman PT-17 biplane. It had a powerful 220 HP radial engine, compared to the 60 HP J-3 Cub I had previously flown: it was a large airplane and a terrific aerobatic ship. "My instructor is a bird, an old-time flyer." Mr. Gilligan was a civilian and very experienced. He was flying Spitfires for the RAF in 1940 and had done all kinds of flying:

barnstorming, the mail, airlines, everything. He loved to fly at night, and nothing was more fun to him than night aerobatics. We learned all types of aerobatics, loops, rolls, Immelmanns, split-S, and others, but only during the day. Night aerobatics were prohibited.

Occasionally when we were on the way home after sunset, Mr. Gilligan would say, "Watch this, I got the aircraft." This meant he was going to fly. I turned over control of the ship and held on while he went through a routine of aerobatic maneuvers, all precise, perfectly controlled, and designed for thrills. He was the best, of course. I was sworn to secrecy, lest the brass find out we were violating the prohibition against night aerobatics.

One other trick he taught me was to land the Stearman while looking at the tail. The Stearman was notoriously difficult to land because of the poor visibility over the nose and its narrow main landing gear. It was an almost impossible proposition to land the thing without looking ahead and using your peripheral vision on either side of the nose.

Mr. Gilligan made it look easy. I was happy to experience his expertise and felt honored to have his trust. He was also a gambler and he won and lost more money during the eight weeks of Primary we were together than I would make in ten years.

I was one of the first in the class to solo the Stearman after just six hours of practice flight. After that, I did a lot of solo practice, mostly taking off and landing, while Mr. Gilligan gambled with the other instructors on the ground. Occasionally he would fly dual with me to introduce new maneuvers and then turn me loose to practice them solo.

If ever there was a time when I absolutely fell in love with flying, this was it. The sense of freedom and control was addictive and accretive. It only got stronger over the years. That first terrifying mission over Austria and many others during the war tested my commitment to being an aviator, but I never wavered.

In May 1943, there were lots of familial events going on in Newburgh, the most notable of which was my older sister Marguerite's pregnancy with her first child. She was due any day. The family and Eleanore were anxiously awaiting the birth. My younger brother, Ed, was sent to El Paso, Texas, to begin his Air Defense Artillery training. The Army had caught up with the pilot shortage and started sending hopeful pilots like Ed to the other branches. The familial goings on made me pretty homesick.

On Mother's Day 1943, I wrote Mom and told her that I missed her and everyone so much. It was funny how certain days, holidays, and birthdays, brought emotions closer to the surface. I also missed Eleanore and she missed me. We were planning for her to come South for a visit during the summer. I finally wrote to the folks on May 15 to let them know I wanted to get Eleanore an engagement ring when she visited. I wasn't sure of the response I would get from Mom, as she still wasn't sold on Eleanore. However, I was mature enough to make up my own mind in such matters.

After 47 hours of flying in Primary, the next step in the Cadet program took me to Basic Flight Training in Newport, Arkansas, the armpit of the world! This was worst place I had ever been assigned. It was muddy all the time, hot and humid, and to top it off, the food was abysmal. The first night almost all the cadets got diarrhea from the food. I know this because when I awoke with horrible stomach pains and went to the bathroom, which was in another building, I met many of them lined up in the mud and waiting their turn to relieve themselves.

During the orientation, we were told that the town of Newport had a population of around 3,000 and had the distinction of having a venereal disease rate three times the national average. There was no reason to go into town.

I met my instructor, 1st Lieut. Levy, who was a decent fellow and a veteran of the China-India Theater, having flown Curtis P-40s there. He took us out to the airfield to look over the airplane we would be flying in Basic. The Vultee BT-13 Valiant was several orders more complex than the Stearman. It had radios, instruments, a 450-HP engine, flaps, and a Hamilton Standard controllable propeller. It had no hydraulic system and the controls were not the easiest to operate. It required a fine touch to fly the required maneuvers smoothly. It was faster and heavier than anything I had flown.

The pilots nicknamed the BT-13 the "Vultee Vibrator." The origin of the Vibrator nickname was unclear, with several different stories credited. My favorite was that on takeoff, the powerful radial engine and adjustable propeller created a harmonic vibration that caused the windows on the base to vibrate whenever a BT-13 took off.

I was a little intimidated by the complexity of this new airplane, and initially it proved to be a difficult airplane to fly. I had a devil of a time landing it, and if Lieut. Levy had not been there a couple of times, I would have bought the farm. After 14 hours of dual instruction, I think Lieut. Levy was frightened of flying with me and didn't know what to do. He said, "Do you think you can do it [solo]?" I popped right back: "Sure thing, Sir," not quite believing myself. "I was tired of fooling around and I decided to do it or else." I did, and my flying in the BT-13 got straightened out after that.

We lost the first cadet from our class in a training accident about this time. He ran into some bad weather on a night cross-country hop. The field had him on the radio and told him to take the airplane to 3,000 feet and bail out, but he decided to make a forced landing. He got out of the weather and found a good area for forced landing, then stalled the airplane making the turn to final approach and bought the farm. This incident was an eye-opener and gloomy lesson for me. I realized that aircraft accidents were seldom caused by one thing, but were usually a sequence of events, any one of which, if interrupted, could prevent disaster. It was a lesson that helped me get through my combat missions later.

I made the mistake of telling my folks about this accident and they started worrying. Finally, I wrote them with youthful bravado, "Whatever you do, don't worry about me, as I'll always come out OK. I am in this racket now and expect to make a living from it the rest of my life. You might as well resign yourself to God's will. I will always try to stay on the ball in my flying as well as my religion and for the rest of my life." As I reread these words, they were probably not very reassuring to my apprehensive parents.

We were so busy every day in Basic, there was little time for rest. Drill, parades, inspections, ground school, flying, and physical training made sure our days were full. There was barely time for sleeping, and when we started night flying, there was even less sleep.

"The officers are hard-nosed and as tough on us as they can be." And I already told you how bad the base and Newport is. It is already getting to 90-100 degrees. Standing at attention outside in this heat always claims a few casualties. If it gets any hotter, I may be the next one! They're trying to find out what kind of men we are. "The threat of washing out is ever-present and contributes significantly to the pressure."

To make my situation worse, in June of 1943, Eleanore got a strep infection and they had to remove her tonsils. I was really worried until she wrote a few weeks later and said everything was fine. In the middle of June 1943, a few weeks before we were to move to the next phase of flight training, we picked up some scuttlebutt that cadet training would be phased out of Newport Army Airfield and it would be turned over to the Marines. Too bad it didn't come a little sooner.

In the BT-13, we did a lot of cross-country flying and a lot of night flying, which I didn't like initially. I became used to it and started to realize the potential advantages. The bad guys couldn't see you and neither could the brass. It was like a free ticket to "cowboy" in the airplane. I took the opportunity on some of my night flights to buzz a few baseball games and other public outings.

While in Newport, I quit smoking for the first time. My throat had been irritating me and I was afraid that it would turn into a cigarette cough. I tried to make it permanent, but eventually the pressures of combat drove me back.

By the end of July 1943, I had completed all my ground school and flight requirements in the BT-13 and could not wait to leave my exile in Arkansas. I received orders to report to George Field in Lawrenceville, Illinois, for multi-engine qualification and Advanced Flight Training. This training assignment made it pretty certain that I would be flying bombers in combat. This would be the final phase of AvCad, and at its completion, I would receive my aviator wings and a commission as a 2nd Lieutenant. To make things even better, Eleanore had the month of September 1943 off and she was planning to spend most of it in Lawrenceville, IL. I wrote my folks again and told them we wanted to get engaged.

George Field made Newport, Arkansas, look even worse than a prison camp. The improvements were dramatic. The fact that we were in the last phase of AvCad entitled us to more privileges and almost no harassment. Also, it felt good somehow to be north of the Mason-Dixon Line. I was on the last lap of "achieving my lifelong ambition" to fly. I began my campaign to convince the folks to come out to my graduation at the end of October.

Eleanore worked out her arrival for August 30 and she would stay for three weeks. "Everything was going so right that I was beginning to look for a catch." Even Mom had resigned herself to my commitment to Eleanore, with the proviso that we wouldn't get married right away. I was intending to give Eleanore the ring during her visit and was fairly consumed with this task during August.

At George, I flew a twin-engine training ship, the Beechcraft AT-10 Wichita. This airplane had two 295hp Lycoming radial engines. It was kind of a crate, but was reasonably fast at 195 miles per hour and it was my first chance to fly an aircraft with a retractable landing gear. Twin- and multi-engined airplanes introduce potentially complicated issues with asymmetrical thrust if/when one engine goes out. A pilot really had to be on the ball to recognize the problem and execute the emergency procedures swiftly. Initially, I had a problem with identifying the dead engine: they don't allow you to look outside to see which prop has stopped. But that was soon overcome and I was among the first to solo after about 12 hours of training.

Before Eleanore arrived, I started getting admonitions from Mom about not getting married while Eleanore was in Illinois. I wondered where she got an idea like that? By late August, she had not sent me the money I had banked in Newburgh to buy the engagement ring. I wondered if it was because she thought that might be an impediment to our doing something foolish. I tried to reassure her that it wasn't going to happen and all but demanded that she send me my money. Demanding was always a dangerous thing with Mom, but she had no idea how committed I was.

When Eleanore arrived, I was flying nights. I was able to get the wife of a friend to meet her. I didn't see her much that first week. "I got her a room where some of the other 'cadet widows' were staying. Real cute." Within the confines of my military duties, we had a great time the first three weeks of September 1943. I had a Class A pass and could leave the base anytime I was off duty.

Of course, the first order of business was to select a ring. I had planned on spending around $150, but that wasn't going to get my future wife what she wanted. I had been through the engagement ring disappointment with my sister, Marguerite, when she got engaged. Her then-fiancé, now husband, Harold, surprised her with a ring. That was a big mistake. The whole family heard about that mistake for a couple of years. I wasn't about to begin the engagement with a disappointed fiancée. We finally agreed on a platinum set ½-carat diamond solitaire for around $200. The ring had to be custom made and would be mailed to Eleanore in Newburgh.

We had such a great visit in Illinois, socializing with some of the married cadets and their wives who lived in the boarding house. We went dancing at the USO Club, played cards, and explored the area around Lawrenceville. You have to love farms because that is all there is around here. It was harvest time and there was a lot of activity, some of it even interesting!

We advanced our relationship by getting to know one another even better. Eleanore wanted to set a date for getting married, the sooner the better. "She said she was coming out to stay with me at the first decent post I'm stationed at. I'm having a hard time holding her off. She says that she is going to surprise me completely when she comes." She didn't want to hear about the uncertainties of Army assignments, potential deployment overseas, my commitment to Mom and Dad about not getting married immediately, or any rational thoughts on the matter.

Emotionally, I pretty much felt the same way by the end of her visit, but thought it necessary that one of us should be anchored in reality. It was difficult to say goodbye when it was time for her to leave. She cried and it was all I could do to not well up. After her train pulled out of the station, I felt empty and figured the best thing to do was to immerse myself in my flying. I wrote my folks that if I got a leave following the training here, Eleanore and I would like to get married at home in Newburgh, "No fuss and no bother."

Upon graduation from AvCad, a newly minted 2nd Lieut. aviator was assigned to a transition school to train in the airplane he would fly in combat. All these schools were on different schedules and spread all over the country. There was no guarantee that I would get any leave after advanced training, and I didn't.

The flying at George was very interesting from many standpoints. First, the Wichita was an advanced trainer. It had all the latest navigation instruments that a combat aircraft would have. Second, the training emphasis was on navigation, finding our way to a point and returning, a necessary task for success in flying bombers, particularly the return part. Third, we learned to fly instruments under the hood, simulating flying in the clouds, and fourth we actually got to go places in the airplane.

We flew to other military bases in Wisconsin, Mississippi, Louisiana, Ohio, and other states. The routes were never direct. We were required to fly over preplanned checkpoints along the route, another vital skill for piloting a bomber. I flew over Lake Michigan, which is black as pitch at night, and then directly over Chicago, which was lit up like a Christmas tree. I might like to do this kind of flying for an airline after the war.

By the end of August, my lobbying to get the folks to come out for graduation had come to naught. Mom said that it might make my brother Ed feel bad if she came to my graduation, but not his. I was pretty disappointed that they were not coming, but Eleanore's visit soon got me back on track.

A few weeks after Eleanore left, I graduated from AvCad on October 1st and was extremely proud to be a 2nd Lieut. and receive my silver wings. The fact that no one from the family was there to witness my occasion hurt a little. As a sidelight, 25 years later to the month, my son John graduated from Army flight school at Fort Rucker, AL and received his silver wings. Eleanore and I were there. John asked me to pin on his silver aviator wings.

I received orders report to Gowen Field, Boise, Idaho, for transition training in the B-24 Liberator heavy bomber, with no leave enroute. I wasn't even able to go home to Newburgh and bask in my accomplishments. I wrote, "Miss you Mom & Pop & Marg & Hats, & Sherman was right when he said war was hell. I miss Eleanore plenty too."

I arrived at Mountain Home Army Airfield, a satellite base to Gowen, via Salt Lake City, on October 6, 1943. Mountain Home was another outpost on the edge of the world. The town amounted to nothing and its surroundings were a good imitation of Death Valley. It was flat, cold, windy, and covered with sagebrush. The place was another disappointment. Beyond just my comfort level, most importantly, it was not "a decent post" where Eleanore might join me.

Mt. Home Field, like all the training bases in the Army, had to produce a quota of pilots and crews to feed the war machine. At Mountain Home, they ran a B-24 transition school for pilots. Everyone began as a copilot in the training. Following the B-24 transition school, the best pilots would be designated first pilots and receive their crews. These new first pilots would then conduct operational training with their crews for a few months at either at Mountain Home or Gowen Field in Boise, 60 miles up the road. Following this, the crew would be considered combat-ready and deployed overseas. Those who were not designated first pilots would become copilots assigned to a crew and go on operational training.

I arrived during a crisis in the Army Air Corps. The big picture was that, beginning in 1943, the United States could not train enough crews to keep up with bomber production and crews lost in combat. Industrial production was outstripping the Air Corps training infrastructure. While we were in a holding detachment at Mountain Home, awaiting transition school, new arrivals were immediately assigned to go up on an orientation flight in the B-24 with instructor pilots. There was no pre-flight instruction or ground school to learn about this complex aircraft.

From what I could determine, these flights were to assess our airmanship abilities. After three or four hours with the instructor, I was told to report to the ops officer, a major, who relieved me of my co-pilot duties and told me I was now a first pilot and would receive my crew in two months. Always the optimist, and believing him to be unaware, I explained that I had not completed the transition course and was not qualified to fly a B-24.

He said, "Lieutenant, I don't give a damn. My job is to put crews together for operational training and deployment. Your job is to do what you are told. Find 1st Lieut. Scruggs and tell him I said for you to ride along with him when he is flying his normal students. You are on your own as far as ground school goes. You got two months before I assign you a crew. Now get the hell out of here."

My word, that conversation was a little bit of a shock! I was altogether uncertain as to whether I was even capable of learning the ground school subjects on my own or mastering flying of the B-24 with tag-along instruction from Lieut. Scruggs. So much for the exigencies of war! Turned out that Lieut. Doug Scruggs had just returned from the European Theater, where he had flown 30 missions with the Eighth Air Force out of England. He was an instructor pilot in the B-24 transition course and a wonderful guy. I went up with him and his students each day, and got some flying time after he had finished with his normal students. That's how I learned to fly and got qualified in the B-24.

Doug assigned me to study a section of the B-24 Pilots Flight Manual each day. He quizzed me before and/or after the day's flight with his other students, who, I should add, had the benefit of ground school. Over the course of two months, it was a race to see whether I could master the big bomber before my crew was assigned. It was a 1940s version of on-the-job training combined with distance learning.

I had managed to accrue 135 hours of flight time in two months, which was more than the actual transition course. I flew at every opportunity, including Christmas Day 1943. I found my situation to be very typical in the service. There was always an imperative to go somewhere or prepare for something and when everything was organized, we waited. "Hurry up and wait" was life in the service.

In late December, they moved me to Gowen Field in Boise, Idaho to assume my first pilot duties and to be assigned a crew. My crew was assigned after the first of the year, including six enlisted men who "were the roughest bunch I had ever seen." Their looks were deceiving. They had been well trained and were courteous, disciplined, and qualified for their jobs.

The Horn crew consisted of

2nd Lieut. John H. Horn, Pilot
2nd Lieut. Fred W. Mittles, Co-pilot
2nd Lieut. Frank Belasco, Navigator
2nd Lieut. Charles (Charlie) Freedman, Bombardier
Tech. Sgt. Harvey H. Ulmer, Flight engineer
Tech. Sgt. Edward Seibert, Rear gunner, waist gunner
Staff Sgt. Allen T. Bunker, Air gunner, ball turret
Staff Sgt. Leonard W. Edsall, Nose gunner
Staff Sgt. Leon M. Glencoe, Top turret gunner and radio operator
Staff Sgt. Edmund D. Duobrowolski, Tail gunner.

Gowen Field met Eleanore's requirements for a decent base. Arrangements were made for her to take the train out to Idaho to get married. When she arrived, the wives of several friends took care of her for a few days until the hastily organized wedding could take place. The Catholic chaplain married us Saturday, January 9, in the base chapel. Because you are reading this you know the marriage worked out pretty well! Eleanore loved the little apartment I had rented. She got straightaway to making it "cute" and we settled into married life.

The only barrier to our marital bliss was Mom Hamway's nervous breakdown about a month after we got married. Eleanore was terribly upset and shocked. She cried for a long time when we received the special delivery letter. We called Mr. Hamway and he said that everything was being taken care of OK and not to come home. He said, "Mrs. Hamway will be herself again in a few months."

By the beginning of March 1944, our crew had completed Phase 2 of Operational Training. We had another phase to complete and then we would be sent to an embarkation point for shipment overseas.

Operational training was demanding, but was also the most fun. We were doing everything that would be expected of us in combat. We flew in formation within a group of several aircraft, albeit many fewer than in combat. We navigated as a formation and every ship had the chance to lead the formation. The crew practiced their gunnery, firing the B-24's ten 50-caliber machine guns on targets being towed by other aircraft. My crew was particularly good in gunnery, lulling us into the fantasy that with all those guns spitting lead accurately, we would be invulnerable to enemy fighters. We did precision bombing practice and even got to drop some live bombs.

A word about formation flying: it was terrifying and I was never comfortable doing it. The concept of airplanes flying in close formation meant that would mass their fire power against attacking fighters. Formation flying was based on the principle of war, "Mass," first revealed by Sun Tsu in his Art of War, an ancient Chinese military treatise dating from the fifth century BC. It made sense, but caused me untold discomfort.

Aircraft were organized for missions into section formations, loosely organized by squadron. The sections were made up of 9-12 airplanes divided into three flights. Each flight of three or four aircraft would fly in either a diamond or a "V" formation.

When flying in formation, planes were completely dependent on the others in the formation to hold their relative position for safety. One wrong move by one plane would be amplified once it was transmitted to the last plane, which could and did result in midair collisions.

Midairs seldom had a happy ending. I had my crew take a little different approach to formation flying. Instead of it being a responsibility of just the pilot and co-pilot, it was the duty of every man on the aircraft to keep me and the co-pilot informed of the position of the other aircraft in the formation. Everyone's head was to be on a swivel, surveying our surroundings. This kept the intercom plenty busy, which in itself could be a distraction, but it was the only way I could fathom to safely fly in formation. The scheme saved our lives many times when a crew member warned me to take evasive action against a wandering B-24 within our formation.

A few words about who the combat airmen were: fighter pilots, bomber pilots, and enlisted bomber crewmen. Curiously, the Army excluded transport pilots from the combat airmen classification. Obviously, there were times when C-47 pilots dropping airborne troops on D-Day or C-46 pilots flying "The Hump" to resupply China resented their exclusion. The genesis of this exclusion was probably that a far greater number of transport pilots were ferrying supplies in secure rear areas and the classification for designating combat and non-combat wasn't very sophisticated.

The vast majority of the 121,867 Army Air Force casualties, including 40,061 killed, were from bomber crews and fighter pilots during World War II. Combat airmen came from all over the United States, were of all ethnic backgrounds, and had all sorts of different civilian occupations. What they had in common was they were all volunteers, they were in the top scoring levels on the Army General Classification Test (GT Test), and they were between the ages of 17 and 27.

There were five categories, based on GT Test scores. Most combat airmen tested at Category 1 or 2, which was considered by the Army to be "high quality manpower." Most of the combat airmen shared a love of flying, in spite of high casualty rates. More than 12 percent of all combat deaths in the Army and 10 percent of all combat deaths among all the services during World War II were among combat air crewmen. Despite the danger, they had higher job satisfaction than, for example, infantry officers (McManus, 2000).

The duty of training my crew was a "real job." I was 23 years old and my experience in leading men, other than in AvCad training, was nonexistent. I found supervising nine men to be daunting. Plus, I felt it was my job to learn and understand all their jobs to properly lead them in combat. My co-pilot had been to the B-24 transition course, but had not proven to be an apt pupil. I literally had to teach him to fly the airplane. Getting the bombs out on time and on target required precise teamwork between the bombardier, navigator, and pilots, and such choreography was not intuitive.

Harvey Ulmer, the senior enlisted man and flight engineer, was a tremendous asset, although at times he seemed to despair trying to teach me his engineering tasks. The radioman, Sgt. Glencoe, quailed at bringing me up to speed on his tasks. The four gunners were pretty proficient. The biggest job with them was restraining them from killing someone who didn't need it. "I could see the crew becoming more proficient. Having three officers and six enlisted men under my command is no mean task. They come to me with all their problems and I have my hands full."

My crew was a cross section of America, hailing from the East coast to West coast. One lesson I tried to instill was that we must take care of each other, because that is all we would have at 20,000 feet over enemy territory. I learned quickly that 2nd Lieut. Frank Belasco was indispensable. He was a college graduate from California and had been an aircraft engineer working at Lockheed when he entered the service. I was able to lean on him to help with decision-making. Harvey Ulmer was a natural leader and became the equivalent of the 1st Sgt. for our crew; I relied on him to interface with the enlisted guys.

Phase three of the operational training focused on long-distance navigation at night. We made flights all over the United States in this pursuit: Spokane, Portland, Reno, San Francisco, and my favorite, Seattle, where we flew by a beautiful snow-covered Mt. Rainier sticking up through the clouds at 15,000 feet. Frank Belasco was absolutely the best. His course plots were spot-on, no matter the weather or winds. I lived in fear that someone with more rank would recognize his abilities and steal him from us.

We received the orders for our crew to leave Boise for Forbes Field in Topeka, Kansas, at the end of March 1944. This was a designated port of debarkation for points overseas, but we still didn't know whether we were bound for Europe or the Pacific or India. These were the places that B-24s were stationed. I wanted to go to the Orient, but that was not to be.

El and I took the train and arrived in Topeka on April 4, 1944. We found a room to rent. There were no cooking facilities, so we ate at the officer's club and generally enjoyed military social life there; dancing, playing cards, and the food and drink. It was a great introduction to the military for us.

Shortly after we arrived, my crew and I were issued the airplane that we would fly overseas and presumably into combat. It was a new B-24J that had fewer than 20 hours. As the pilot, I was required to sign for the airplane, and I don't mind saying how intimidated I was to assume responsibility for this $300,000 piece of equipment. At the same time, I felt a surge of delight and a tremendous pride of ownership that the Army entrusted me with it.

This huge machine was our ticket into and out of combat. From that day forward, whatever airplane we were assigned came first. We didn't quit until the airplane was ready to fly the next day. Following every flight, we combed over the ship to find and fix any irregularities. The officers pitched in beside the enlisted crew, which turned out to be a tremendous team-building experience and not necessarily the norm. The Horn crew agreed: if we didn't make it, it would not be because we failed the airplane or for a lack of teamwork.

My Eleanore at Bear Mountain, 1943.
Collection of John H. Horn.

Nashville Classification Center, 1943.
USAF via author.

My Academic Record in Preflight.
U.S. Army form via author.

Group picture at Mr. Lisenby's home.
Collection of John H. Horn.

Boeing-Stearman PT-17 Kadet primary trainer.
Wikimedia.

Vultee BT-13 Valiant.
Via author.

Beechcraft AT-10 Wichita.
Via author.

AAF Training Command Pilot School graduation, George Army Airfield. Via author.

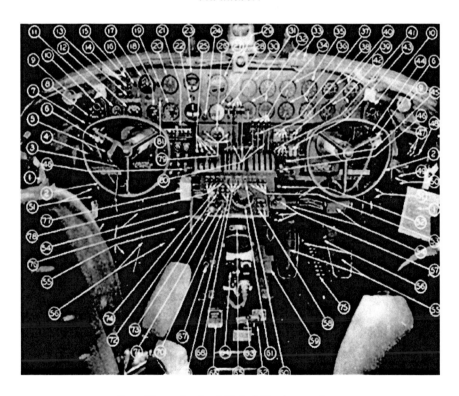

B-24D cockpit. USAAF via author.

Chapter 3

The Road to Weiner-Neustadt

WE were sure proud of that airplane, U.S. Army Air Forces B-24J, SN 43-0021, built by the Ford Motor Company at its Willow Run factory in Michigan. The B-24 was the most produced airplane of all time, with 17,000-plus units manufactured. It is an injustice that even though more B24s were produced and they could fly higher and farther and carry more payload than the B-17, they never received the same recognition. The high-wing design and the placement of the B-24's fuel tanks throughout the upper fuselage and wing, and its lightweight construction designed to increase range and optimize assembly line production, made the aircraft more vulnerable to battle damage.

It could be a beast to fly and was sternly unforgiving. At times, it took all the strength two men could muster to control it. After long missions, I was so exhausted that sometimes the crew had to help me out of the pilot's seat. The B-24 was notorious for its tendency to catch fire, which was a constant worry. Its high, fuselage-mounted, very efficient Davis wing also meant it was dangerous to ditch or belly land, since the fuselage hit the water first and tended to break apart.

Nevertheless, the B-24 provided excellent service in a variety of roles, thanks to its large payload and long range, although it did not have the survivability of the B-17. It was the only bomber in World War II to operationally deploy the U.S. forerunner to precision-guided munitions during the war, the 1,000-pound Azon guided bomb.

Finally, we were told we'd be deploying to Italy to join the 15th Air Force to a place called San Pancrazio. Eleanore and I made arrangements to give up our living quarters and for her to return to Newburgh while I was overseas. It was a pretty gloomy few days as we made the preparations to be separated. We said goodbye at the Topeka train station on April 12. It was one of the saddest days of my life. Our leave-taking was no different from that of millions of other couples. Anyone who has ever gone to war can attest to the melancholy that overcomes because of the uncertainty of ever seeing loved ones again.

We departed Forbes Field on April 13 and flew a circuitous route thru Florida, Trinidad, Brazil, and North Africa via Senegal, Algeria, Morocco, and Tunisia (see Appendix A). We landed at San Pancrazio, Italy on May 13, 1944. We were flying as one of a chain of several B-24s, each separated by several miles, across the ocean. The navigation had to be perfect and Frank was up to the task. As we crossed the coast of Africa, we were heading straight for the airport in Dakar, after a 2,000-mile trans-oceanic trip!

There was only one hiccup on the trip. While in Fontelza, Brazil, we got together and named our ship The Merchant of Menace, which was a play on words of Shakespeare's play, The Merchant of Venice. Frank designed some very clever cartoons depicting Shylock riding a bomb. We chipped in and hired a local artist to paint the bomb-riding Shylock on the nose, as well as the names of all our wives and girlfriends, on the outside of the airplane by our crew stations. We even had leather patches made for our flight jackets. This entire process was a huge morale-building activity for the crew; we were very proud of that ship.

Our takeoff time from Fontelza was midnight on April 19. The aircraft was loaded, the mission planned, and we strapped into the airplane around 1130. We initiated the checklist and started the APU. Once we had electrical power to the ship, I cranked the #1 engine and it refused. After several tries, the ops officer gave us the order to unload the Merchant of Menace and reload into the next new B-24 down the line. Sadly, we never saw The Merchant of Menace again.

San Pancrazio, which we called San Pan, was originally a German airfield surrounded by a small base. The recent Google Earth photo of the runway shows two distinct surfaces. The darker surface on the northwest end of the runway was the original German runway. The much longer, lighter portion of the runway was the extension the USAAF built. The perimeter of the base was greatly enlarged, requiring the requisitioning of several civilian houses and barn buildings. This included the Scarpello family home (See Appendix C) and barn.

San Pan was a typical Army Air Force airfield and installation among the dozens between Foggia and Lecce. It consisted of OD tents for sleeping, a few slapdash wooden frames covered by canvas for meals, and requisitioned masonry buildings for the headquarters, operations office (ops), and officers club. It was hastily organized and erected, as were dozens of others, as soon as the allies were able to establish security south of the Gustav Line. The boot heel area of Italy was never heavily occupied by the Germans, as the rest of Italy was. However, they did use the area to acquire food and supplies.

When the Americans landed on the mainland around Salerno, the Germans withdrew from Southern Italy to behind the Gustav Line with little conflict. Following the war, the requisitioned stone buildings reverted to their Italian owners and still existed in 2015. The actual airfields ranged from concrete to pierced steel planking (PSP) to hard-packed earth. San Pan had a little of each.

San Pan was the home of the 376th Bombardment Group (BG), nicknamed The Liberandos, and was the unit to which we were assigned. There were four squadrons in the 376th (511th, 512th, 513th, and 514th) and we were assigned to the 513th. The 376th BG was one of the most storied units in the entire USAAF, having participated in the first low-level raid on Ploesti, led by Medal of Honor winner Colonel John "Killer" Kane. This raid started the Battle of Ploesti that was to rage for more than a year. For a complete history on the 376th, see http://www.376hbgva.com.

The 376th BG was one of several BGs and fighter groups (FG) belonging to the newly formed 15th Air Force in December 1943 (Tillman, 2014), operating principally out of airfields between Foggia and Lecce. The mission of the 15th was to open up the underbelly of Nazi Europe to the Allies' strategic bombing campaign. This had been impossible on a large scale until the

Allies gained a foothold on the Italian mainland because of the flying distances from bases in Africa or England. With air bases in the boot heel of Italy, all of Europe and the Balkans became accessible to the B-24s, with their 2,000-plus mile range.

In January 1944, General Jimmie Doolittle, of Doolittle's Raiders fame, turned over command of the 15th Air Force to Major General Nathan Twinning. By that time, it had 37,000 men and 1,100 crews to man the 739 B-24s and 200 B-17s and hundreds of fighters. The 15th Air Force organization chart at the end of this chapter clearly shows the dimensions and complexity of the air effort from Italy. It was a huge undertaking, with tens of thousands of men flying thousands of aircraft from dozens of airfields.

The concept of the strategic bombing campaign as divined by the American and British planners was to destroy Germany's ability to wage war by bombing industrial, transportation, and other targets employed in the war effort. This concept later morphed into breaking the morale of the enemy populace by bombing population centers. The American and British employed slightly different means to this end.

The British believed that night area bombing was the best way to execute the strategic bombing campaign. The Americans believed that daylight precision bombing was best way to execute the concept. The apparent lack of concern for civilian casualties and collateral damage in the strategic bombing campaign seems strange today. And the only reason fathomable is that the very existence of civilization as we knew it was believed to be at stake.

History has a way of repeating itself, and the 15th Air Force occupation of the boot heel of Italy was not the first time foreign armies had occupied the area. One of the classic historical clashes, the Battle of Cannae, was fought here in 216 B.C. on the south bank of the River Aufidus, 35 miles southeast of Foggia. Two Roman generals, Lucius Aemilius Paullus and Gaius Terentius Varro, had 48,000 infantrymen and 6,000 cavalrymen posted there. The Carthaginian leader, Hannibal, had 35,000 infantrymen and 10,000 cavalrymen.

When the Romans attacked, Hannibal allowed his forces to fall back and spread out until the Romans had pushed deep into the center of his forces. The Roman army was convinced that the Carthaginians were retreating. They were not, and the Roman penetration allowed Hannibal to bring his rear guard around and envelope the Romans. The Romans were defeated soundly and without mercy. It was the largest defeat in the history of Rome, with approximately 54,000 Romans killed (Mark, 2011). It was in this historical backdrop that the 15th Air Force settled in for their own battle.

In the first half of 1944, the immediate operational mission for the 15th Air Force was to gain and maintain air superiority in Europe by destroying the German Luftwaffe. This was essential to make Operation Overlord (D-Day), scheduled for June 1944, possible. Roosevelt, Churchill, and Stalin agreed that air superiority was essential for Operation Overlord to be successful. Consequently, in the first half of 1944, air superiority had a higher priority than the strategic bombing campaign. The destruction of the German ability to wage air war prior to the invasion, by dispersing the Luftwaffe fighter forces between the French, Russian, and now Italian fronts and by destroying their means to prosecute the air war (aircraft, aircraft factories, airfields, fuel refineries, and other war industries), became the highest priority.

To give an idea of the complexity, sophistication, and level of effort of the 15th Air Force attack on the German air forces, a description of one mission mounted in March 1944 follows.

In March 1944, Luftwaffe fighter strength had reached a total combined strength of 235 planes at Aiello, Lavariano, Maniago, Osoppo, Gorsia, and the Udine airfields in Northern Italy astride bomber routes. The Luftwaffe was seriously challenging Allied control of the sky over northern Italy. In response to the challenge of gaining and maintaining air superiority in Italy, the 15th Air Force dispatched its largest task force to date, with a total of 592 planes in a well-coordinated attack to neutralize these airfields and destroy the maximum number of enemy fighters in the air and on the ground.

First, three groups of P-38s—95 planes—were sent on a low-level strafing mission over these airfields, avoiding enemy radar and effectively holding enemy aircraft on the ground. At the same time, a group of 113 B-17s made a feint toward Germany as though they were headed to targets in Germany. That movement of bombers flushed up fighters in the Klagenfurt and Graz Austria areas. After their feint, the B-17s turned west toward the Udine and Villaorba airfields, where they dropped fragmentation bombs. Fighter escort for the B-17s downed seven Me 109s and other types of Luftwaffe aircraft that had been scrambled to intercept them from the Klagenfurt and Graz.

When the B-17s finished their bombing runs on the Italian airfields, the German fighters from Klagenfurt and Graz areas that had been chasing them, began to run out of fuel. This scenario had been anticipated by our 15th Air Force planners. These Luftwaffe fighters had to make emergency landings at the bombed airfields or alternative fields nearby. These fighters from the Klagenfurt and Graz area were now concentrated on the ground at Gorzia, Lavariano, and Maniago aerodromes (A/D) now. This was in addition to the normal complement of fighters already assigned to the fields.

Now three task forces of B-24s consisting of 260 bombers dropped 32,370 fragmentation bombs on the massed enemy fighters on the ground. Only two enemy planes were able to get off the ground to relative safety (Capps, 2004; Tillman, 2014). As described, the operational concept was complex and required precise coordination and timing. Considering the relatively primitive equipment available, that such missions could be mounted and be successful is remarkable.

Under the scenario of gaining air superiority before D-Day—although unknown to almost everyone—we arrived in Italy to pick up our part of the war. Between the map of Italy and the photo of San Pan, one can get an orientation of where we operated. The place was hewn from ancient olive groves, and judging from the deeply rutted roads, looked as if it were just drying out from the winter rains. The temperature was very pleasant, in the 70s.

We were quickly in-processed and assigned sleeping arrangements in large general-purpose tents. The officers were billeted separately from the enlisted members of the crew, so I made a special effort to ensure that my enlisted crew members were set up at least as well as their contemporaries. The senior enlisted man on our crew, Harvey Ulmer, guided me to where our guys were billeted. We did a short inspection tour and I was well satisfied.

In reality, the enlisted tents had been improved by their residents, with pallets used for flooring, homemade heaters using 100-octane aviation gas, electric lights, and other amenities. They were better than the officer's tents and exhibited all the knowhow and ingenuity of the American G.I. My brief walk-through inspection made it clear that the best way to get something, out of the supply system or otherwise, was through my enlisted guys.

Before supper that night, we all received Army field equipment, steel helmets, packs, canteens, and a mess kit, which consisted of two metal trays that folded together with a knife, fork, and spoon inside. We ate out of them every day, three meals a day, and were responsible for washing them after each meal. We had three strategically placed garbage cans of hot water, soapy water, and rinse water. Failure to wash these properly usually resulted in a case of the runs, a particularly unpleasant scenario when the bathroom was outside and 100 feet away from our sleeping tent or when we were 20,000 feet in the air!

In-processing included medical checkups and shots, malaria briefings, sanitation, and the ubiquitous and very graphic Army film on venereal and other sexually transmitted diseases. The dos and don'ts of living on the base and circulating in the community were briefed by the military police (MPs). The Chaplain, Father Jim Murphy, introduced himself and his services. The finance people were next, to pay us, and the administrative section did our personnel records in-processing. At this point, the crew was split up: the enlisted men went with the first sergeant, an imposing, balding man from Texas whose name was Cash.

The officers went to the ops building where we all sat down and waited to meet the group commander (CO), Lieutenant Colonel (Lt.-Col.) Theodore (Ted) Q. Graff. He entered the room and we were called to attention. All stood, ramrod straight, until he gave us the "at ease."

Graff was a mustachioed man of average size who looked older than his 40-something years. He was direct and his presentation was short and sweet. "School's out," here in the ETO (European Theater of Operations), he said, "This is the real war. If you want to survive this mess, follow orders."

He went on to say, "The ops officer speaks for me with regard to missions and flying. Take care of your enlisted crews and listen to your NCOs (non-commissioned officers, the sergeants). Make sure that the airplane you are flying—and it will most likely be a different one every mission—is ready to go: check, check, and double check it."

Finally, he told us that his door was always open if we had anything of a personal nature to discuss. His stern attitude and demeanor drove me to promise myself I would never take him up on that offer. Abruptly, he summarily left the room before we could jump to attention again.

With in-processing out of the way, we settled into camp life and awaited our first mission. The days came and went and the Horn crew wasn't called. We were all anxious and eager to do what we were trained for and to find out what combat flying was all about.

The officers in my crew and I attended the daily mission briefings just to get a feel for what was going on and to practice planning the missions. We planned each mission as if we were going: routes, flight times, fuel required, all the details. This paid dividends later, as once we started flying, we were better prepared than the other new crews were and we had heard all the stupid questions, so we were saved this embarrassment.

After chow on May 15, the following day's mission assignments and crews were posted on the bulletin board. We were on it! For security reasons, crews were not told what the mission would be or where the target was until the briefing, just minutes before takeoff. In the morning mission briefing, we were told the target would be the oil fields at Ploesti. Wow, our first mission would be to the infamous Ploesti! Our practice attendance at the mission briefings enabled us to fit right in and avoid all the inane and unnecessary questions of a "newbie" crew on their first mission. The mission ended up being a non-starter: we were turned back after a few hours because of the weather at the target.

We were alerted for a mission the next day, on May 17. Takeoff time was scheduled for 1030. We had breakfast around 0730 and went to the mission brief at 0930 and were told that the target was the harbor at San Stephano, Italy. The weather, route, harbor layout, and expected enemy resistance, including anti-aircraft and fighters, were briefed.

Each pilot was given a mimeographed sheet with the position of each aircraft in the formation, routes, IPs for bombing runs, altitudes, inter-plane radio frequencies, and call signs. The bombardiers received a separate sheet pertaining to target recognition, expected winds aloft, bomb ballistics, fusing, and interval data. All airplanes had ten 500-pound bombs with variable timing (VT) fuses set for detonation 300 feet above the target.

VT-fused bombs, set to explode above the ground, were designed to take out soft targets such as personnel, vehicles, and ships. Point detonated (PD) fused bombs were designed to destroy hard targets like armored vehicles, bunkers, and underground infrastructure. The gunners were given a special briefing on enemy fighter tactics and on testing and firing their guns. Everyone was briefed on escape and evasion procedures. Lt. Col. Graff gave us a few words and the briefing officer gave us a time hack to synchronize our watches.

The flying uniform in sunny San Pan was the normal wool shirt and trousers, heavy wool socks, sheepskin-lined pants, and jacket over the wool uniform. A sheepskin hat with ear flaps covered our heads and ears. We also carried our steel helmets, which we donned over the target to provide some minimal protection to our heads from flak shrapnel.

The sheepskin jacket and pants were heated by plugging them into receptacles in the airplane, a system that had about 50 percent reliability. We must have looked ridiculous in all this clothing in the southern Italian spring. However, the temperature at the altitudes we were flying frequently dropped below 10 degrees in the summer and it was much worse in the winter months. Without these clothes, survival was impossible. Frostbite was the most common injury among combat airmen.

For security purposes, start, taxi, and takeoff all took place while observing radio silence by using colored flares. We took off at one-minute intervals and had to watch for the aircraft in front of us in the formation so we could take our position. It is a commonly accepted axiom in flying that landing is the most demanding task. Flying a combat-laden B-24 turned that upside down.

The published maximum gross combat weight for the B-24 in the operating manual was 56,000 pounds. This was regularly exceeded and our aircraft were as heavy as 71,000 pounds. With up 3200 gallons of 100-octane fuel, bombs, flak vests, extra ammo, and all manner of other equipment, every takeoff was a thrill on San Pan's 4,800-foot runway. It took the airplane 4,200 feet to accelerate to the takeoff speed of 110-120 mph, and pilots had to make a determination of whether the airplane was going to make this speed by the 3000-foot point in order to have enough runway to abort the takeoff and stop.

It was not unusual for heavily laden B-24s to crash on takeoff, with awful fires and casualties. I was never inclined to allow my copilot to handle this demanding task and I always flew on takeoff. I tried to share the other flying equally between us, but Fred was happy for me to do the majority of the flying.

Above 10,000 feet, all of the crew members were required to wear oxygen masks. These were rubberized affairs that smelled and never quite fit comfortably. Because of the extreme temperatures at altitudes up to 28,000 feet, the masks sometimes froze up, rendering the unlucky crewman unconscious, or if not discovered in time, dead from anoxia.

The mission to San Stephano was routine. "A good job was done," as Harvey Ulmer wrote in 1944. We ran into some light but accurate flak. There was no damage to our plane. We arrived back at base around 1615, having flown five hours and forty-five minutes (05+45). We were all pretty excited about logging our first combat hours of flying and too dumb to be scared.

The ground crew picked us up at our airplane in a 6x6 truck after a thorough post-flight check and delivered us to debriefing. Debriefing was conducted by the intelligence staff, who sought to learn all they could from the crews about the enemy and the defenses in the mission area, and importantly, any observations of friendly aircraft that had been shot down. Debriefing was mandatory for every crew member and was never a routine affair. We got two ounces of whiskey during the debriefing, ostensibly to calm our nerves.

I was alerted after the evening meal that we were tasked for the next day's mission. The mission briefing was scheduled for 0630 with takeoff at 0730. Those times indicated that wherever the mission took us, it was to be a long flight. The May 18 mission turned out to be Ploesti again. Ploesti supplied 60 percent of Germany's crude oil requirements from their oil field and refinery complex. It was seen as a center of gravity for Germany's prosecution of the war and the Allies had been attacking it since June 1942 without conclusive results.

As mentioned previously, the 15th Air Force, and specifically the 47th Bomb Wing, including the 376th, staged one of the war's most daring low-level bomber raids on Ploesti in 1943, and it had been trying to finish the job ever since. Shortly after dawn on August 1, 1943, 178 B-24s took off from bases in Libya and headed northward toward the heavily defended Ploesti, 1,000 miles away. The formation flew at 50 feet of altitude to avoid radar. The mission was led by the 98th Bomb Group and its legendary commander, Col. John R. "Killer" Kane.

Clouds over Bulgaria separated the B-24 formations and the integrity of the bombing elements became disjointed. The formations had not only been tracked by radar, but eavesdropped on by the Germans since takeoff, who had broken their communications code. The B-24s arrived over the target at treetop height without the planned element of surprise. Despite intense defensive fire from the ground and from the Axis fighters, the armada pressed the attack.

Overall damage to the target was heavy, but the cost was high. Of 178 planes and 1,726 men who took off on the mission, 54 planes and 532 men failed to return. The heavy casualty rate was a combination of the enemy's readiness, the disjointed American formation, and poor timing. Some of the American casualties were caused by delayed-action bombs dropped several minutes previously by their own bombers. That was the last low-level raid on Ploesti. As later reported by Barron (1996), Col. Kane was awarded the Congressional Medal of Honor for his courageous leadership in this action. Dozens more high-level precision raids, many of which we participated in, followed until August 1944, when the target was ultimately considered destroyed.

The day's mission was to bomb one of the most heavily defended Axis installations in Europe. The good news was that we were to get credit for two missions toward the 50 required to get back to the States. Ploesti was considered among the most dangerous targets in the ETO. Takeoff at 0730 and formation of the group's 38 aircraft over the airfield was routine.

Once the formation was complete at 5,000 feet, Maj. French, the group leader, led us to rendezvous with two other 47th Bomb Wing groups (449th, 98th) assigned to this mission. The 449th was to lead the wing and we (376th) were to follow them over the target, with the 98th in trail. There were roughly 120 B-24s in the formation attacking Ploesti this day. Once the wing was formed, the lead group began a slow 250 feet-per-minute (fpm) climb to the 19,000-foot bombing altitude.

We flew northeast across the Adriatic Sea and the weather began to deteriorate to the point of a solid overcast beneath the formation over the target area. Because the bombardier was unable to see the target, we could not drop the bombs. The flak was moderate, but inaccurate. We suffered no damage.

As we turned southwest, toward San Pan, it dawned on me that we would be landing with 5,000 pounds of bombs on board. It wasn't long before the crew started an intercom chat on the topic, which was soon monopolizing the airplane intercom system. I was as concerned as they were, but took comfort in the fact that landing with bombs was routine and there was no option. I gave the word for the crew to cut the chatter and keep their eyes open and their heads on a swivel. Our outbound fighter escort never materialized and I was thankful that it wasn't needed.

We (Fred, co-pilot; Frank, navigator; Harvey, engineer) talked over the landing of the bomb-laden B-24 at San Pan. We discussed the expected longer braking times and nose heaviness, among other things. It was a worthwhile exercise because it took some unexpected muscle to raise the nose in the landing flare. I compensated for the heavier landing weight by touching down in the first few hundred feet of the runway in anticipation of longer braking distances.

The brainstorming idea we used to solve this problem was a process I used frequently to address the unfamiliar. I was proud of how we solved this problem; it showed a certain maturation of us as a crew. We arrived back at San Pan at 1245, for a total flying time of 05 + 15. Our first trip to Ploesti was anti-climactic, based on everything we had heard, seen, or read about it. We did not know what to think—it seemed too easy.

Per the usual procedure, the mission sheet was posted outside the mess tent and we were up again for the following day's mission on May 19. Harvey commented, "Looks like they are trying to wear us out," (Ulmer, 1944). We were awakened at 0300 for the mission. The briefing was at 0445 and takeoff was at 0545 to bomb La Spezia Harbor on the west coast of Italy. We encountered a little heavy-caliber flak, sustained no damage or injuries, and were "feeling pretty lucky now." We had P-38 and P-47 fighter escorts and "sure felt good with them out there."

Our next mission, mission 5, was May 23 to bomb troop concentrations just southeast of Rome in Frascati, Italy. This was the rear area of the German Army in Italy, behind the Gustav Line. Destruction of the target would reduce Germany's ability to reinforce the Gustav Line.

From the target at 18,000 feet, we could see the historic buildings of Rome. The thought of dropping bombs that close to Rome and potentially destroying icons of Western civilization gave me serious pause. I am thankful we never were assigned the mission to bomb Rome. The city was actually bombed on several occasions in 1943 and 1944, primarily by the Allies and to a lesser degree by Axis aircraft, before the city was taken by the Allies on June 4, 1944. In the 110,000 sorties that comprised the Allied Rome air campaign, 600 aircraft were lost and 3,600 air crew members died; 60,000 tons of bombs were dropped in the 78 days prior to Rome's capture (Katz, 2003).

Flak at Frascati was heavy-caliber, but not intense. Great visibility over the target enhanced its accuracy. We suffered no damage or injuries and logged 05 + 00 hours of flight time.

This story began with the narrative of mission 6/7 to Weiner-Neustadt On May 24, 1944. It was a tough one—our crew's baptism by fire—and one we never forgot over the course of our tour. This was the mission that made veterans of us. We flew an old B-24D from when the unit was activated in Libya in 1943. The 376th suffered the loss of several ships, shot down by heavy accurate flak and German fighters. From the ships that were able to return to San Pan, many crew members were killed and wounded. Our ship had no injuries, but it suffered more than 30 holes and Harvey said, "I was scared as hell" (Ulmer, 1944). Getting credit for two missions was little consolation for the terror we endured.

It's a remarkable fact that during World War II, an Army infantryman was sent overseas to fight "for the duration." Combat airmen were overseas in the war until they completed 50 missions in 1944. In my case, that was less than five months. At one point in 1943, combat crewman in the Eighth Air Force flying from England only had to complete 25 missions because casualty rates were so high.

The Army calculated the number of missions to tour completion based on casualty rates. As the Allies gained air superiority, the casualty rates for air crew members declined and the number of missions to tour completion increased. Even though the Army's data on casualties didn't necessarily support it, I felt my lot in the war was better than most. I had a warm cot, hot meals, regular mail, and a shorter overseas tour, all of which were far more than ground forces had.

At the macro level, I was serving all those back in the States—Eleanore, Mom and Pop, and everyone else—and helping our country claw back the sense of security and pride that we lost at Pearl Harbor. I was contributing in a meaningful way to the war effort, and if I survived, cementing my livelihood after the war.

By now, you know how I ended up at Weiner-Neustadt on May 24, 1944. It boiled down to a lifelong love of flying; luck, with some bad and some good; and a young man's determination to be a part of the defining event of the times: The Great Crusade. Mission 6/7 taught me that I didn't like being in the war—it scared the hell out of me. The incredible violence of air combat, mechanical malfunctions, accidents, and unsanitary living conditions all combined to make me wonder how anyone made it home.

I still enjoyed flying, when not terrorized by the enemy, and was good at it. My reputation was building in the unit as a reliable, safe, and steady aircraft commander whose crew was well prepared. Fortunately, no one knew the overwhelming fear and in my heart and the disquiet I felt when leading my crew into the crucible of combat. I guess that was a good thing. Keeping my own counsel in these areas was vital to being an effective leader. Keep reading and find out how I got out of the mess.

2nd Lt. John H. Horn's crew.
USAF via author.

Aerial view of San Pancrazio today. The runway used in 1944
is still intact and can be seen at upper center.
Google Earth via author.

Scarpello farm house as it stands in 2015.
Author photo.

513th Squadron patch.
376th Heavy Bombardment Group Inc. via author.

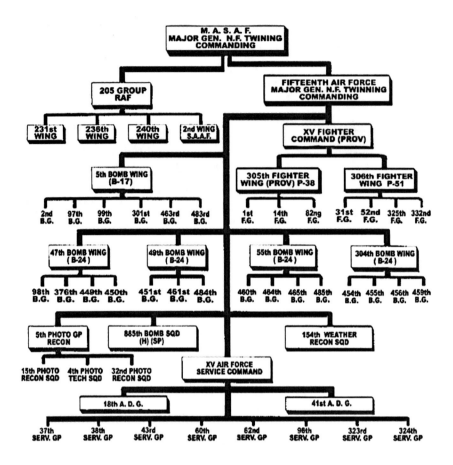

15th Air Force Organizational Chart.
15th Air Force web site via author.

Army mess kit.
Via author.

Preparing for a Mission at San Pan.
Sergeant Fred Felty via author.

Chapter 4

The Grinder

AFTER that first trip to Weiner-Neustadt on May 24, time seemed to shift into slow motion. I was conflicted between being involved in every mission so I could get to 50 quickly and go home, and being on the wrong mission at the wrong time and not getting home. A sort of rotation was established by operations so each crew got about the same amount of flying time. It was possible to get additional flying by volunteering to fill in on other crews. Obviously, we didn't have a choice of which missions we would fly and we didn't even know what the mission was until shortly before takeoff.

In a classic case of no good deed goes unpunished, the decision makers in the 513th squadron wanted the best crews on the riskiest missions. Sometimes we could get an idea of how bad the mission was going to be by the crews who were scheduled. Everyone knew who the best pilots were, and if they were all scheduled, it was going to be a rough one. Taking all this into account, I decided not to be a volunteer, but to take each mission as it came down from the decision makers and to stick with my crew. Some of the guys on my crew did volunteer for the extra missions, and in one case this ended in tragedy. Most of us were happy to stick together and take whatever missions we were assigned.

All combat air crew members were volunteers, and as such, could "un-volunteer." Crew members could refuse to fly missions, but that was usually the end of their careers in the Army Air Corps. The recalcitrant would disappear from the unit post haste, probably to serve in the infantry.

Aircraft commanders had a bit more leeway and could refuse an airplane for maintenance faults, but this was a rarity. If aircraft were available, two spare B-24s would crank with the airplanes scheduled for the mission. If one of them became inoperative during the cranking and run-up, a spare aircraft would take its place on the mission. If the spares were not needed, the crews shut them down and went back to bed.

Anticipating 43 more missions before getting my ticket home was a daunting prospect. It was unmistakably clear what we were up against now and it wasn't going to be easy. We got a day off after Weiner-Neustadt and it took me all day to unwind. After chow, I sidled over to the mission board and saw we were on the mission sheet for May 26.

I wasn't completely confident of my own readiness to go out again, but put on a brave face and passed the word on to the crew. We were assigned to bomb the rail marshalling yard at Nice, France. This was briefed as a maximum 15th Air Force effort and several bomber wings would be in the area. The briefing was at 0400 and takeoff was scheduled for 0530. Our airplane, #8, an older B-24D called Elsie, was parked at the farthermost point on the airfield. After cranking the engines, we attempted to taxi out, in turn, to the runway.

Unbelievably, the modern B-24 did not have a steerable nose wheel: it was a castering affair. Steering was accomplished by differential engine thrust and braking. To make things worse, the pilots could not see the main landing gear and had to depend on the flight engineer, from his position sticking up through the forward escape hatch, to relay the aircraft's location with regard to the edges of the taxiway. Taxiing the behemoth was not quite an exact science.

Elsie was parked at the end of the line and we had a long taxi on this day. It was dark, the surface changed from hard-packed dirt to PSP to hard surface, plus we had crosswind. None of this made taxiing it any easier. As I jockeyed the throttles and brakes to conform to the engineer's directions and the centerline, the airplane was all over the place, eliciting yawns and snide remarks over the radio from the other aircraft waiting to depart. The derision was merciless, but good-natured. I was glad when the flight leader reminded everyone that we were supposed to be maintaining radio silence.

The sun had barely broken the horizon when we finally took off. The day promised to be beautiful and we were going to the much-vaunted French Rivera! The serenity of the dawn sky was in sharp contrast to the violence of the war. Nice was 800 miles or so and this was going to be a long day.

The 30 bombers of the 376th formed over San Pan, made a slow turn west northwest, and began a 250-fpm climb to 18,000 feet. Our fighter escort of P-38s joined us about 100 miles from the target. They protected us to where the flak started and then waited for us to emerge from the target area. Over the target, we met some moderate heavy-caliber flak, but we received no damage. We saw no fighters on the way out of the target area. Total flight time for the mission was 08 + 30.

We had many Italians working in our camp at San Pan, and of course, we initially were a little suspicious of them. After all, they were our enemies until their capitulation in September 1943. They were hired to perform all the menial tasks that were essential to deployed armies: laundry, handling all the garbage and human waste from the outhouses, cleaning, serving, boot polishing, barbering, tailoring, and eventually even cooking.

It was up to the group adjutant, Capt. Charlie Piraneo, who was an Italian immigrant at 9 years old, became an American citizen at 16, and attended West Point. He was a native Italian speaker whose family spoke only Italian at home. Charlie created and ran the local national employment program.

There was no shortage of workers. The Italians at this time had nothing: What was not destroyed was appropriated by the Germans as they retreated up the peninsula, from livestock to fine art. Living conditions for the residents of San Pan were absolutely wretched and a job on base was a lifeline. In many cases, it meant that the family would not starve. All sections in the squadrons submitted worker requirements and Charlie did some creative pencil work to document the positions.

Locals were prohibited from working anywhere near classified information, but other than the ops office and headquarters areas, they were everywhere else. All workers had to be vetted as to their security status. Some of the jobs, such as sanitation workers and food handlers, required continuous health monitoring. The flight surgeon's aid station tent was always full, performing these checks.

Charlie was also charged with all the hiring and firing. In current culture, Italians are sometimes stereotyped as lacking a work ethic, but in those days, there was no lassitude among them. As an impoverished, defeated people with nothing, they were completely reliant on these jobs for survival. They worked hard and were always ready to do more. The entire local national employment program was a huge responsibility for a 26-year-old captain with a degree in civil engineering. The talented Capt. Piraneo was always busy with the program and his talkative Italian workforce. Everyone from beggars to the mayor of San Pancrazio visited him. In the eyes of the locals, he was the most important man on the base.

Each officer's tent had a maid to take care of the four to six residents. The cameriera (Italian for maid) or camis, as we called them, were women of varying ages and degrees of attractiveness. The cami's job was to wash our clothes, keep the tent cleaned and organized, shine shoes, and generally perform as a house maid and valet. For these invaluable services, the camis were paid ten dollars a month, a huge sum to the Italians in those days.

There were a lot of hormones running wild among the young pilots and some of the camis did extra duties for additional remuneration. This, of course, was prohibited, and if discovered, the cami would be fired and the offending serviceman would be disciplined.

Our cami was Isabella, or Izzy, as we called her. On the scale of Italian femininity, with Sophia Loren being a 10, poor Izzy was a 1. She was painfully thin and singularly homely and thus didn't attract the interest of any of the hormone-crazed men. She was able to devote all her energies to her principal duties. She was super-efficient and took pride in her guys having the shiniest shoes and the cleanest and most finely pressed uniforms.

She was old to us, probably about 34, widowed, and raising three young children. The wages of each category of worker were set and all the camis made the same salary, but we did all we could to help Izzy and her family with additional resources: treats for her kids, leftovers from the mess hall, and other items we could find. When I told Eleanore about Izzy, she started including small things for Izzy's children, such as a pair of socks, small toys, and other sundries when she sent me a package.

The camis were assigned to a set of living quarters; tents, in our case. The occupants came and went, but the cami stayed with her assigned quarters. Changing a cami was usually requested for a wrongheaded reason, such as extracurricular activities. It took an act of Congress to change your cami because it set up a chain reaction that affected all the camis and residents. Charlie frowned upon changing cami assignments and could usually convince the requester that it was in his best interest to leave well enough alone.

Scuttlebutt was that a few airfields up north had experienced sabotage of their aircraft on the ground. Suspicion naturally fell on the Italian workers. The 376th never experienced any security problems with the Italians on base. In mid-June, the 376th received a squadron of Black soldiers (we called them colored troops) to maintain a 24-hour guard on the aircraft. These security troops were commanded by the White group security officer. Other than being on the flight line together, the colored soldiers were kept completely segregated.

Segregation was a new experience for me. Growing up in Newburgh, we went to school, played sports, and lived next door to all races, including Blacks. The security squadron was a very professional group of men and very interested in the goings-on of the 332nd Fighter Group, known as the Red Tails. This was an all-black P-51 fighter group, stationed up the Adriatic coast at Ramitelli Airfield. I was happy to tell them that we were frequently escorted to and from our targets by the Red Tails and had never lost a bomber to enemy fighters while under their protection. It was true that the Red Tails saved our bacon more than once, as did the other fighter squadrons in the 15th Air Force.

On May 27th, the mission was to bomb the railroad marshalling yards in Marseille, France. This was to be another long mission. We had a fighter escort of P-51s from the 332nd and had no trouble from enemy fighters. We were in Elsie again and the flak over the target was particularly vicious. Flak damaged and jammed the rudders and our #1 engine, which had to be shut down. The rudder was jammed in a position that made the bomber want to turn left. This required that we use differential power to counteract the damaged rudders in order to keep the nose more or less lined up with the direction of flight.

The procedure for shutting down an engine involved the flight engineer placing himself between the pilot and copilot seats. One of the pilots, in this case, me, called out each step on the checklist and the flight engineer executed that step and responded. For example, the first step was, "Identify the bad engine." The flight engineer would respond: "#1 identified." The most critical step was to actually shut down the faulty engine by closing the throttle and mixture levers, turning off the magnetos, and feathering the propeller so the blades would be streamlined.

Miscommunications in the fog of war caused more than one airplane to be lost because the flight engineer shut down the wrong, properly working, engine. Had the wrong engine been shut down with our jammed rudders, already requiring max power from the #2, it would have been fatal, and I was particularly vigilant during this process.

When we got #1 shut down and secured, I started thinking about how and where we were going to land the airplane. With the rudder jammed, the airplane would not streamline in the direction of flight. We were in a permanent left yaw or crab. It took both Mittles and me to hold the controls to counteract the asymmetrical thrust. The net result of using the controls and engines to keep the airplane streamlined was the airplane was in a cross-control situation reducing our speed considerably. We powered back #3 and #4 to reduce the pressure on the controls which slowed us down even more and fell behind the formation, making Elsie prime Luftwaffe bait. Thank God for the P-51s, who stayed with us until we were well out to sea.

In the air, the yaw condition did nothing more than slow our speed. Landing in a yaw would cause real excitement though.

Once the wheels touched down, the airplane would shoot off the runway in the direction of the yaw.

I asked Frank the location of the nearest longish runway with good emergency equipment and he recommended Naples, another six hours away. Harvey, Frank, Fred, and I discussed ditching the airplane close to the coast versus landing it. The B-24 was not noted for its robust airframe and, unlike the B-17, whose low wing would cushion a water landing, the Liberator would touch down fuselage first and most likely be ripped apart. Crewmembers would certainly be lost.

In the end, we chose Naples: and staying dry. The next decision was whether to land on the wheels, which would provide a little more directional control on the runway, but would chance a misalignment (with the runway) on touchdown causing a landing gear to collapse, spinning the airplanes around and igniting the inevitable conflagration. The other option was to do a belly landing, which was sure to cause enough friction to ignite the airplane, but would stop us sooner. We knew Naples had the best fire rescue capability in Italy and that the fuel tanks would have several hundred gallons remaining. Based on the idea that a wheeled landing would cause the least friction and least chance of fire, I made the decision to land with the gear down. Unfortunately, it would also require the finesse of a brain surgeon to do it correctly.

When 30 miles out, I declared an emergency and the tower at Naples scrambled the emergency vehicles. Per our SOP, I directed the crew to secure themselves in their crash stations. On approach to landing, we slowed the airplane to the minimum controllable airspeed using full flaps. We were on the verge of stalling or the airplane rolling over on itself. This exacerbated the asymmetrical thrust and the airplane yawed even more to the left.

Mittles and I were fighting against the controls to keep the airplane steady. Just as we were about to touch down misaligned, I cut the power on the #3 and #4 engines while leaving the #2 at full power. The nose of the airplane started around to right, and when it was lined up, I planted the big ship on the runway and pulled the power off #2. On rollout we used the engine's power to keep it straight until we had slowed enough to use differential braking to steer the bomber to a safe halt.

Just as we came to a stop, the left landing gear collapsed with a clunk, the wing hit the ground and it deformed. Fuel started pouring from it. I shouted over the intercom to "get out", turned off all the electrical power, and followed as the crew jumped, crawled, or leapt out of the crippled ship. Elsie didn't ignite, but she never flew again.

The Lord was with us that day. We logged 09+00 hours on this mission, 9. It felt like a lot more. The squadron commander recommended me for the Distinguished Flying Cross for superior airmanship. It was later awarded by the Group commander (See Appendix E).

We spent the night in Naples and were picked up by our unit the next day in the 376th ash-and-trash ship. It was interesting to see how the other half lived in the more permanent facilities at Naples. They had a fabulous officers club, with all the booze, cigarettes, and food a guy could want. They had real hot water showers and flushing toilets.

Lots of guys relaxing in the club were accompanied by beautiful Italian women. There was no dust or mud and everyone looked clean. This was very unlike our existence at San Pan, where everything and everyone was coated with a film of dust. We really had everything we needed there and I decided that life this close to the flagpole didn't suit me. Nice place to visit, but wouldn't want to live there.

We had a day off. Our next mission was scheduled for May 29th, to the dreaded Weiner-Neustadt to bomb the A/D again! It was an early mission and the briefing was at 0430, with takeoff at 0530. I couldn't eat much breakfast for the trepidation I felt. We were assigned a brand new B-24 that had not even been named yet. The crew chief hovered over us, checking and rechecking his new steed until it was time to crank.

We picked up P-51 and P-38 escorts on the way into the target area. The flak was accurate and intense and damaged several ships. It looked to me that we did a pretty good job of destroying the A/D, but it had been done before and the thing kept rising from the rubble.

On the way out of the drop area, when we were clear of the flak, the formation was jumped by Me 109s. The fighter escorts immediately engaged the attacking aircraft, but were outnumbered and a few German fighters got loose. The Me 109s flew head-on at the group formation and used their cannons effectively, shooting down two aircraft and badly damaging another.

We were in the middle of the 2nd Section and had a fearsome view of the charging Me 109s and their cannon shells as they whizzed by us in the formation. Several crew members were WIA from the flak and fighters. We were among the lucky and sustained only multiple holes and rips in the skin of our aircraft.

As a formation, we made a right turn out of the target area, drawing the fighters farther away from their bases, and finally managed to get out of their fuel range. With several holes in our brand new B-24H, I was cheerless to take it back to the crew chief, despoiled as it was, knowing that it would hurt him more than it hurt us. We logged 08+00 hours and this was mission 10/11 for us.

We were not on the flight schedule for May 30. It was hard to sleep in when multiple bombers were taking off. Even when we were off the flight schedule, we usually were up drinking coffee, smoking, and watching the flight depart for the day's mission. Only two sections of 26 airplanes were flying today.

As an aside, during training, the B-24s the young pilot trainees took off in never weighed more than 56,000 pounds. Then they came to the war and started flying combat missions. I said earlier that takeoff was always an exciting experience on the 4,800-foot runway. In addition to routinely carrying up 8,000 of pounds of bombs, we had 3000 plus or minus gallons of hazardous, aromatic 100-octane gasoline on board, thousands of rounds of ammunition for the guns, more ammunition for the two guns in the plane's waist, flak suits and helmets, and our heavy flying clothing. It was not usual to take off weighing more than 68,000 pounds. The record in our group was calculated at over 71,000 pounds.

During takeoff, an engine failure or malfunction would mean crashing in a flaming mass at the end of the runway or shortly after. An error in the pre-takeoff checklist—flaps not down twenty degrees, engine cowl flaps not closed, or control locks not unlocked—meant that we would not fly, but become a huge fireball.

When fully loaded, if we didn't have a headwind to help us, it took almost the entire runway just to get off the ground. It took a 4,200-foot takeoff roll on our 4,800 foot runway to accelerate to the necessary takeoff speed of 110 to 120 mph. Inattention to the engine performance, aerodynamics of the airplane as it gained speed, or heavy handedness on the controls during the takeoff roll had disastrous results.

2nd Lieut. Rob Mitchell's crew was short a ball turret gunner on the day's mission. Staff Sergeant Allen Bunker, from my crew, volunteered to fill the vacant position, flying in #93, Bubbles, an old D model. Allen had been grounded the day of our first mission and was anxious to catch up with the rest of our crew in terms of missions completed. The mission was to the Pottendorf aircraft factory, just east of Weiner-Neustadt, and it promised to be dangerous. Harvey Ulmer really didn't want Allen to go and said so to me. He said that Allen should be resting with the rest of us. When I asked if he wanted me to step in and be the bad guy to disallow Allen to volunteer, Harvey said "No," but this would be the last time he would allow anyone to volunteer.

Allen was from Neenah, Wisconsin, and right off the farm. He was of German descent and had worked on the family dairy farm practically since he could walk. When he was 15, his parents pulled him out of school and put him to work on the farm full-time. He loved farm life, and frequently regaled us with missives about animal husbandry, crops, and the like.

Before he settled down permanently on the farm, he reckoned that he wanted to see the world. World War II provided him the opportunity, and at 17, he enlisted in the Army Air Corps and volunteered for combat air crewman training. Allen joined our crew in at Gowen Field in January 1944, shortly after turning 18. He was a bright light, very enthusiastic, polite, and always willing to assist us "old guys."

I was watching the 29 bombers depart for the mission that day, not taking any particular note of the airplanes. The last bomber in the first section, #93, was accelerating and the nose lifted at the correct point, but just before liftoff, the airplane seemed to hesitate. The nose came slamming back down to the ground, shearing the nose gear and plowing off the runway through the ground. The front section of the bomber was crushed back to the wing roots and immediately caught fire. Emergency vehicles were scrambled and all of us watching ran for the crashed aircraft to lend assistance.

My heart sank as I ran to the burning aircraft. It was #93 and Allen was inside. I looked up and saw the tail gunner shimmy out of his broken turret and thought, "That's one," and said a short prayer of thanks. Regretfully, the tail gunner was the only crew member who escaped, and he was almost uninjured. With 2700 gallons of AVGAS burning, there wasn't much anyone could do. The heat was so intense that those without protective suits could get no closer than 100 yards to the fiery wreckage. Sgt. Allen Bunker was immolated in the fire, along with the remainder of the crew, and he was listed as KIA.

The shock of losing Allen had a terrible impact on the entire crew, but on no one more than on Harvey and me. It was ultimately my acquiescence that allowed Allen to volunteer for the mission. Harvey was the senior enlisted man on the crew and although he didn't feel right about Allen volunteering, he let it go.

I didn't know it was possible to feel this terrible, and I don't mind saying that I shed some tears for our loss of Allen, as did the other crewman. After a few hours of tears and thought, I spoke with Harvey. We commiserated about the loss. We agreed that it was important to honor Allen's death, but also to get past the loss in order to remain effective as a crew for the remaining 40 missions. We resolved that volunteering was no longer an option for our crew. Doing what was required of us as a team was hazardous enough, and allowing our team to volunteer for more was something we as leaders could not live with.

The 376th group chaplain conducted a memorial service for the crew of Bubbles, as was the custom. Harvey and I decided to conduct a private service just for our crew. Each crew member was given the opportunity to say something about Allen. I felt a need to own the responsibility for Allen being in harm's way and said so to the crew. I disclosed our new no-volunteer policy and did not get any flak from the guys.

A few of the guys told humorous vignettes, some said prayers, and some said nothing at all. Frank Belasco talked of our future as a successful crew and about how Allen would have wanted that. He was poetic. Being able to talk about Allen was healing and enabled us to go forward into our tour of duty. Losing Allen was one of the saddest events in my life, and the worst I have ever felt.

On May 31, we were selected for another tough one, mission 12/13 to Ploesti, to bomb the Romano-Americano refinery. This was another 15th Air Force max effort and the raid tasked five bomber wings plus two fighter groups for the mission, more than 600 airplanes. If I haven't said so before, Ploesti was the third most heavily defended Axis target, after Berlin and Vienna.

It was an early 0330 wakeup with the usual scrambled powered eggs or gluggy oatmeal breakfast, both of which could be had with Spam. When we got to the briefing room, everyone saw the red yarn stretched from San Pancrazio to Ploesti. If anyone was still sleepy, that thin red string got his full attention. The mission brief was the usual, with emphasis on the stiff opposition expected. We rode out to our plane, #47, a B-24H named Little De-Icer, around 0500 and began our pre-flight to make sure the airplane was sound enough to stake our lives on.

Takeoff was 0600 in radio silence. The colored flares signaled the precise time each box of airplanes was to start their engines, and the sleepy airfield came alive with the roar of 120 Pratt & Whitney radial engines. The group's takeoff was orderly, with each aircraft 45 seconds behind the one ahead. We joined up with the group leader, proceeded to take our places within the formation, and departed on course at 160 mph and a 250-fpm rate of climb. The rate of climb was reduced between 15,000 and 20,000 feet because some of the heavily laden ships couldn't keep up. We had one aircraft scratch and return to base for a gas leak.

The route to Ploesti was carefully controlled by the navigators to avoid known flak concentrations. P-38s and P-51s joined us around 0830 for escort, but that did not prevent scores of Me 109s and Fw 190s from attacking aggressively. Bullet holes punctured our wings, but there was no sign of fuel leaking. The B-24 was the first bomber to have self-sealing fuel tanks, and short of a major puncture from a 20mm cannon or large piece of shrapnel, the system worked.

All around the cockpit, 20mm cannon shells burst and shrapnel tore through the greenhouse and aluminum skin around me. This caused a lot of flinching and the corresponding corrections. These deviations were occurring throughout the formation and each round of enemy fire exaggerated them. The drifting aircraft within the formation quickly made me realize that the danger of a mid-air collision was greater than the danger of being shot by enemy fire. I barked for the crew to keep their heads on a swivel and to warn me of encroaching aircraft. The enemy knew full well that causing havoc in the formation was just as deadly as their bullets.

On this day, air combat was as intense as any we had experienced so far. Flak in the target area was heavy and accurate. Several ships were damaged and had to leave the formation to limp home. The formation had numerous WIA casualties due to flak and cannon fire. Only one ship from the 376th was lost to enemy fire. Two ships made forced landings in Italy at American bases north of San Pan. The stiff enemy resistance and smoke over the target impeded the accuracy of our bombs and ensured this would not be our last trip to Ploesti.

The crippled 376th formation arrived over San Pan around 1230 and proceeded to land. My sense was that we had lost more than one aircraft over the target, but that was not the case. Ulmer (1944) wrote, "It is the closest we have been to not getting back." This was counted as mission 12/13 and we logged 07 + 45.

June 1, 1944 was a stand-down day for the entire group. Stand-down days were devoted solely to maintenance of the aircraft and equipment. There were no missions and no flying other than the ash-and-trash ship. It was a welcome respite from aerial combat for crewmen and it was a much more relaxing atmosphere for everyone. All hands, including officers, were expected to pitch in with the maintenance tasks. The crew chiefs particularly enjoyed these stand-down days because it gave them the chance to lord over the officers and direct them to do specific tasks.

On stand-down days, a special evening meal was usually planned. Cookie pulled out all the stops and had the Italians do the cooking that night. The ingredients were the same Army rations as we had every day, but it was wondrous what the Italians could do with them using spices and garlic. I credit the Italian cooks we had with kindling my life-long appreciation for garlic. Mom never used it!

The Italians prepared lasagna with meat sauce, a wonderful salad using dandelion leaves and other weeds, fresh bread, and finally a dessert they called a flan, which was a lot like mom's custard. It was the best meal I had eaten since leaving the states. The Italians particularly prized the jobs in the mess hall because they were never hungry, like 99.9% of their brethren. They always aimed to please. The weather stunk on this particular day and we probably would not have flown in any case.

June 2 was our next mission, to the Simeria marshalling yard in Romania. We had a takeoff time of 0500 so we had 0230 wake-up and the usual breakfast. I couldn't take the eggs or oatmeal and settled for coffee and that great Italian bread. As soon as we washed our mess kits and stored them, we walked to the ops building for the briefing.

There seemed to be a lot of rail equipment concentrated at Simeria. It was used mainly to resupply the German Army on the Russian front and our bosses wanted it destroyed. Resistance in the target area in terms of fighters or flak was briefed as light. I had learned by this time that, although the Germans could no longer mount a sustained high level of resistance across the area of operations, they could mass their forces at a given time and place to mount deadly opposition to our bombers. Thus, a target that was briefed as posing little threat could end up being a hornet's nest on a given day.

Light resistance was always taken with a grain of salt and I never allowed the crew to accept this expectation. My mantra to them was, "Prepare for the worst, hope for the best, and always be ready for a gunfight!" It was safer to be pleasantly surprised at light resistance over a target than surprised by the opposite.

Today the briefers were correct; this was a milk run. I saw one flak burst 10,000 feet below us. We had P-51 and P-38 fighters as escorts and they had no opposition either. They peeled away for their home base as we crossed the Adriatic coast of Yugoslavia. Many of them began an aerobatic show, which made me wish I was in fighters and yearn for my days doing aerobatics in the Stearman. We flew 07 + 30 hours and I was astonished to learn later that we were given credit for two missions (14/15).

More and more I began to feel like a veteran. We had completed 30% of the required 50 missions, experienced the most dangerous targets, had a few close calls, and lived through some war stories to share. In short, what we had to look forward to was more of the same. We had been in country for about a month, and assuming the operational tempo we had experienced was typical, we might be going home in September.

It was a leadership challenge to keep the crew on their toes, avoid shortcuts, guard against complacency, and remain professional. In all honesty, my biggest leadership problem was my co-pilot, 2nd Lieut. Fred Mittles. He wasn't a natural pilot, so I had to watch him like a hawk in the airplane, lest he do some damage or kill us. He was in charge of the last-minute preflight with Harvey Ulmer, while I did the final mission planning.

Feedback from the crew was that Fred was disinterested in this task. He was also a bit of a hypochondriac; always an ache or pain that seemed to come on about the time there was work to be done. I give him credit for being unfazed by the danger and performing well in combat. It was the mundane, routine, but essential tasks where he fell short.

We were both second lieutenants, as were Frank and Charlie, and even though I had a right, as the aircraft commander, to pull rank on him, I found it uncomfortable. My style and preference was to work collegially with all the crew. Fred made it very difficult. The leadership lessons I learned from Pop, about being patient, providing clear explanations, and quietly insisting on performance, were put to the test with Fred and they mostly worked. Thank you, Pop.

On June 4, 1944, General Mark Clark and his 5th Army entered Rome after five months of tough fighting. Clark had been ordered to bypass the city and cut off the retreating German Tenth Army. He disobeyed these orders and instead paraded through the city, playing the conquering hero. The Germans had long vacated the city and no resistance was encountered. The BBC reported in 1944 that the escape of the German Tenth Army, which was significantly facilitated by Clark's insubordination, was responsible for doubling the Allied casualties in the Italian campaign.

We were oblivious to the American forces entering Rome on June 4th and were on our way to bomb railroad marshalling yards near Genoa. It was a multi-wing mission with hundreds of 15th Air Force bombers involved. The routes and timing were even more critical than normal and took the formation across the Italian peninsula to Naples, northwest across the Mediterranean Sea to fly over the northern tip of Corsica, and north to the Italian mainland near Genoa.

The northernmost bomber units departed first and our take-off was scheduled for 0715. We would be the last group over the target and could expect the defenses to be alert and warmed up for our arrival. By the time we got to the target around 1015, the large caliber German 88 (black puffs) flak had zeroed in on the bomber formations. Four of our group's bombers were damaged, but none was lost. Our group consisted of 38 bombers and all but two were able to drop their bombs on the target. Two aircraft had bomb release or bomb bay door malfunctions. We got our bombs off and sustained no damage or injuries from the flak.

The B-24 had a new type of bomb bay door, very similar to the tambour on a roll top desk. The bombing procedure was that after passing the IP and on final approach to the target, the bombardier would open the bomb bay doors and they retracted into the sides of the airplane. He then released the bombs at the appropriate time and closed the bomb bay doors.

When the doors were open, gusts of additional outside air would rush into the aircraft, chilling the already freezing crew and creating significant aerodynamic drag. If the doors were stuck in the open position, the airplane could not keep up in the formation because of the drag. These doors were one of the most troublesome parts of the B-24. Everyone had or would experience bomb bay door malfunctions. On this day, the second aircraft had a bomb release malfunction, which meant the doors opened, but the bombs couldn't be released.

The normal fix for this failure was to have a crew member step down onto a 9-inch aluminum plank (catwalk) that ran the length of the B-24 and was a major structural component, similar to a keel in a boat. This put him between the bomb racks and directly in the face of freezing, hurricane-force winds. Once in position, the crew member would pry, twist, bang, hit, or whatever was necessary to drop the bombs over the target. This worked, mostly.

When it didn't, the doors were closed and the bomber landed with the bombs, or in the case of an otherwise disabled bomber, additional attempts were made over the sea to salvo the bombs. Aircraft #2 was able to get the doors closed and salvo the bombs over the Mediterranean. We ran into heavy and medium-caliber flak adjacent to the target area, but sustained no damage or injuries. We had P-38s escorting the formation and saw no German fighters. We did a good job on our target, the terminus of two major rail lines: the Marseilles-Riviera and Mt. Cenis Lines. Our assigned aircraft that day was a new B-24J, which had never flown a combat mission. It was a sweet bird and I was proud to bring it home to the crew chief undamaged. We logged 08 + 30 hours on mission 16.

June 6, 1944, was D-Day for Operation Overlord, the Allied invasion of continental Europe in Normandy, France. This was the long-awaited operation to lift the yoke of German occupation in France and make the final push to defeat the Germans. The largest amphibious operation in history didn't go as smoothly as hoped and was not a sure thing for the Allies until D + 3.

Once again, on June 6th, we were oblivious of the goings-on in Normandy and were assigned to bomb Ploesti. Maintenance was able to provide only 36 ships. This was another a maximum effort and all four bomber wings of the 15th Air Force were assigned to this mission. We hoped the other units could muster their full complement of bombers. This was a two- credit mission that would count as 17/18.

As usual, the target area was heavily defended by both fighters flak. We were attacked by both Me 109s and Focke-Wulf 190s (Fw 190s). It was the most intense fighter activity I had seen to date. We had P-38 escorts and they were all over the German fighters. It was an absolute circus: The German fighters flying head-on thru the bomber formations while our escorts calculated ways to intercept them. The flak over the target was heavy-caliber of moderate intensity and reasonably accurate. Miraculously, we received no damage from either fighters or the flak. Sgt. Leonard Edsall, our nose turret gunner, sustained frostbite to his legs and feet. Harvey volunteered to replace him. We brought Ed back in the main fuselage behind the flight deck, which was marginally warmer. The flight surgeon diagnosed his injuries as serious and he was grounded for a few days.

Harvey was the kind of guy every commander wanted to have around. He could do almost any job on a B-24 crew and was always willing to step up. I never had to ask for a volunteer because Harvey munificently beat me to the punch. And not only was he that way on my crew, but he was always willing to help out other crews. He had been designated a check engineer, one who checked the others out and frequently flew with other crews when we had a down day.

I looked him up in the 70s when we moved to Sebastian and he was living in Melbourne, FL. He hadn't changed a bit; still the outgoing, competent, courageous, and generous soul I remembered. 30 years had separated our wartime experiences from this visit, but it was if that time did not exist, such was our ease together.

We logged 08 + 00 hours on this trip to Ploesti and lost one ship behind us in the formation due to the heavy flak. Despite multiple raids, Ploesti was still a dangerous place.

After a couple of days off, we were alerted for a mission on June 9 to the aircraft manufacturing facilities in Munich. Our wing, the 49th Bomb Wing, drew the task of bombing the BMW factory, where they built the engines for the Fw 190, among other things. We had an early briefing and take off time was 0500.

We drew a B-24J, #46, No No Cleo for the mission. Preflight, taxi and takeoff went well. It was only when we got over the Adriatic and tested our defensive guns that we discovered that four of the ten machine guns were out. One of the waist guns "ran away" and put eight holes in the rudder. A run-away gun was one that did not stop firing when the trigger was released.

We had been briefed that we might face enemy fighters from Regensburg, Nurnberg, and the Weiss area; all told, more the 380 potential fighters. We had a fighter escort, but we didn't know what unit it would be. Our position was on the left perimeter in the rear of the formation, making us vulnerable to a direct attack. After I digested all this, I made the decision to abort and return to base. I informed the flight lead of my decision and the reason. He agreed and we turned back for San Pan. We logged 05 + 30 hours and actually received credit for the mission, our 19th.

On return to base, I had a come-to-Jesus meeting with the crew chief and his flight chief about the disappointing condition of the machine guns. They were surprised, genuinely embarrassed, and appropriately contrite, and they resolved to never allow the problem again. I made the appropriate notation in the logbook, which grounded the airplane for combat missions until the guns were repaired. I did not take my complaint any farther, but I heard later that the line chief excoriated the crew chief mercilessly and threatened castration if it ever happened again.

As it turned out, the mission was pretty difficult. No airplanes were lost, but many returned with damage and WIA crew members. Was this another Divine intervention for us?

On the next day, June 10, we were on the mission sheet to bomb the Trieste oil storage facilities flying Little De-Icer. The briefing was scheduled for 0415 with takeoff at 0515. The flight to the target was routine. We saw some Fw 190s and Me 210s, but they apparently had other priorities because they didn't attack us and simply flew by at 15 miles distant. Good thing too, as we had no fighter escort this day.

The weather was ideal, what we called "clear, blue, and 22" or CAVU (ceiling and visibility unlimited), which meant clear with no clouds, blue sky, and more than 20 miles visibility. The target was lightly defended and we obliterated it with the no damage or injuries. We logged 07 + 45 for this mission, making 21 for us.

Mission 22/23 on June 11 was to bomb the oil refineries at Constanta, on the Black Sea coast of Romania. This was farther than the Ploesti and the Simeria refineries we had previously bombed and the farthest east we had ever flown. It was another early takeoff, at 0530. We were assigned to fly No No Cleo again and I asked Harvey to be sure that the guns were in good shape on the preflight. He said they were and the subsequent tests over the Adriatic validated it.

We had P-38s escorting us, which was probably why we didn't have any enemy fighter contact. The flak over the target this day was wicked: heavy-caliber and accurate. Several airplanes in the formation were damaged and crewmen injured. Our plane sustained no damage or injuries. One airplane was lost, #33, Big Marge, or so we thought. We logged 07 + 45 on this mission.

After a few days off the mission sheet, we were tapped for mission 24 on June 14 to bomb a refinery near Zagreb at Sisok, Yugoslavia (now Croatia). This was a relatively short flight for a change: it was less than 600 miles one way. Everything was as easy and safe on this mission as it had been difficult and dangerous going to Weiner-Neustadt. It was a total milk run: no fighters or flak. The enemy was absent as we flew over the target, wreaking havoc. The refinery was destroyed and we flew 06+00 hours, arriving back at base at 1315 hrs.

No one in the entire unit had missions on June 15 due to poor weather. On the 16th, the 376th participated in a maximum effort to destroy a refinery on the Danube at Bratislava, Czechoslovakia (now Slovakia). My crew was initially scheduled to fly this mission, but was scratched because the airplane we were assigned, Vivie, could not be made ready in time. The crew and I were disappointed, because we had never seen the famous Blue Danube.

The mission turned out to be disastrous. Initially the 376th had three bombers return early for various mechanical malfunctions, reducing the formation's defensive firepower. At the target area, the German fighters and flak were ready for the marauding American bombers. Three ships and 30 crew members were shot down over the target. Many more ships were badly damaged and had to limp home.

We all had friends on the downed ships and their loss was devastating within the unit. We were extremely fortunate to be scratched from this mission. I knew of the concept of survivor's guilt, but I honestly felt none of that. Everyone in the unit deeply regretted the loss and the impact it would have on the crew member's families. My number could be up tomorrow; I was accepting and thankful that the Lord was watching over us that day.

The 376th needed a rest. It was minus seven (three lost and four that needed extensive repairs before flying again) bombers and unit's morale was in the toilet because of personnel losses. The Wing commander took the 376th off the line and scheduled a maintenance stand-down until June 22: Five whole days with no combat missions.

Still feeling a training deficit, I took the opportunity to fly every day to increase my proficiency in the B-24. I volunteered to fly some of the new pilots on their local area orientation flights. We also received five new and one very well used B-24 that had to be prepared for combat missions, in addition to repairing those we already had.

During the stand-down, we had regular meal hours and, again, Cookie and the mess team made the meals just a little better. It was a break for his mess team to be on a normal schedule and not be required to have food ready 24 hours a day. He was regularly using the Italians as cooks now and the overall chow situation had improved significantly.

We now had a mess tent to eat in and tables to sit down at. We were still using our mess kits, but the Italian waiters now washed them for us. The commander organized some sports and other activities during this time, which was a welcome break from the monotony. We also had a visit from some Red Cross Doughnut Dollies.

These were American women who were working for the American Red Cross and whose sole purpose was to improve morale among the troops. They got their name because they sometimes brought doughnuts on their visits to the troops. They were the highlight of the stand-down for me. To see fresh-faced young American women out here reminded me so much of Eleanore, home, and what we were fighting for. I didn't speak to any of them that day; it seemed enough for me just to be around them.

By June 22, 1944, the 376th was ready to go back to war. During the stand-down, not having to worry about a mission the next day had been calming and relaxing. The unit's airplanes were ready, and more importantly, there was palpable improvement in the morale of the 376th.

We were tapped for the mission on June 22, to Casarsa in northern Italy to bomb a railroad bridge in Vivie, the same airplane that was not flyable for the mission to Bratislava. You can bet that we went over that airplane with a fine-toothed comb. I talked to the crew chief about the engine issues that had prevented it from flying earlier. He said that the power recovery turbines on the #2 engine had been replaced and Vivie was fine. She was an older ship, but looked to be well maintained.

The briefing and takeoff were normal. It was a long flight and the weather deteriorated as we flew north. In the target area, there was 50% cloud coverage, which was borderline for a target as small as a railroad bridge. Charlie didn't think visibility on the target was sufficient for accurate bombing, but the flight lead made the decision to press the attack. There was very little flak in the area and it wasn't accurate. I could not see where our bombs fell and Charlie said he couldn't either. Of this, Harvey Ulmer (1944) wrote, "The job was a lousy one." We logged 07 + 30 hours of flying. This was mission 25, which meant we were halfway to our ticket home!

I was feeling elated about being at the halfway point. I had been overseas for about five weeks and was already halfway there. I just hoped and prayed that the next 25 missions would fly by at the same pace and that we had a few more like today, with minimal enemy resistance.

We had the day off on the 23rd, when the 376th participated in a maximum effort to Ploesti. The mission went well and no planes or crew members were lost. About the middle of the day, too early for the flight to return from the day's mission to Ploesti, I was in a canvas chair getting some sun at the base of the control tower. We heard a bomber in the distance headed our way. Presently a B-24 appeared over the horizon. Lo and behold, it was Big Marge, the aircraft we had lost on June 11!

Apparently, she had been severely damaged, but managed to land behind Russian lines in the Ukraine. The ship needed extensive repairs, for which the Russians had neither the expertise nor the spare parts. The crew was stuck until the 15th Air Force could get the men and materials to Russia for the repairs.

In the meantime, according to 2nd Lieut. Larry Sierk, the crew was stuck with the Russian Army, who treated them very well. He reported that the Russians had little that was appealing in the way of food, but plenty of vodka, which they took the opportunity to drink as much of as possible while grounded. Larry also reported that the Russians had brothels for their soldiers that were populated by women who had been taken prisoners and forced into prostitution. He vehemently denied that he or the crew went anywhere near them, but took some good natured ribbing anyway.

On June 24, the unit was again scheduled to bomb Ploesti and my crew was on the mission sheet. This day only our wing, the 47th, was involved. Referring to the organization chart in Chapter 3, you can see that the 47th Bomb Wing had four groups: 98th, 376th, 449th, and 450th. The Germans held a particular grudge against the 450th, nicknamed the Cottontails because of their white painted rudders. The back story of the grudge goes like this.

Axis Sally said in one of her nightly radio missives that if American bombers ever got into trouble, they could let the landing gear down as an indication of surrender. Luftwaffe fighters would cease the attack and safely escort the bomber to the nearest German airfield. Sometime later, one of the Cottontail bombers was severely damaged as it came off the target at Regensburg, Germany. It could not keep up with the formation. Luftwaffe fighters swarmed in for the kill when the pilot slowed his aircraft, put his flaps down, and dropped his landing gear.

The German fighters backed off, except for two, when they saw his wheels down. The two remaining fighters slowed up to fly close formation with the crippled Cottontail bomber, leading it to the nearest Luftwaffe base. It was alleged that the Cottontail pilot saw the two German fighters near his plane as sitting ducks for his gunners. He took advantage of the situation and ordered his gunners to shoot down the two remaining enemy fighters, which they did easily. If true, the pilot's impulse was shortsighted and even dishonorable, for which many following him in the 450th paid dearly. One of the enemy pilots bailed out and told the story.

That evening Axis Sally announced that Luftwaffe fighter pilots were going to destroy all Cottontails planes for breaching the established protocol. From that time on, the 450th was a fighter magnet. Luftwaffe fighters cruised up and down our long line of 15th Air Force heavy bomber groups, looking for the Cottontails. They would pass up the rest of our bomber groups and zero in first on the Cottontails, with the intent of shooting their entire formation out of the sky.

Currier (1992) reported in his book that in six months, the 450th Cottontails lost 110 planes, while the 449th group flying along with them lost only 63 planes. Rudder markings of the entire 47th Wing, the 98th, 376th, and 449th groups as well as those of the 450th were changed in an attempt to deceive the Luftwaffe. Thanks to the excellent German spy network, Axis Sally, according to Capps (2004), announced the new markings each time a change in rudder markings was made, and the Luftwaffe continued its concentrated attacks on the 450th.

Needless to say, it was providential that we, the 376th, were in the same wing as the 450th and flew together often, which meant much less Luftwaffe attention for the rest of us. German fighters went after them with a vengeance and the remainder of the formation was spared from at least the initial attack.

The briefing for this mission indicated we were to mop up the remaining facilities at the Ploesti oil refinery. Interestingly, the intelligence estimate for enemy resistance was the same as the previous day's mission. This gave me pause to wonder just how much of a mopping-up action this mission would be. The 450th would be leading the formation, so that was good for us.

Taxi and takeoff were routine. The flight had an assorted bomb load: incendiary, fragmentation, and bunker-busting. We had 50 100- pound incendiary bombs fused to detonate on impact. Only 5,000 pounds of bombs and a shorter trip and less fuel meant that we were a little lighter than usual. I gave Mittles the nod for the takeoff and he did fine.

We had escorts of P-51s and P-38s and we needed them. A hundred miles from the target, we ran into unrelenting Luftwaffe Me 109s and Fw 190s. They shot down several airplanes, including two from the 376th. My gunners got three confirmed damages to enemy fighters. As we approached the target area, the enemy fighters backed off and the heavy-caliber, intense, and accurate flak commenced.

Cloud cover effectively masked the target, so I didn't know how much damage was done. Another two aircraft were shot down as a result of flak. We experienced a few shrapnel tears in the skin of our ship, but nothing major. On the way out of the target, a lesser number of enemy fighters returned to harass us. One ship crashed on landing at San Pan, but the crew escaped uninjured. Overall, this was the worst mission yet in terms of losses, but my crew's luck was holding and we came out relatively unscathed. We received credit for two missions (26/27) and logged 07+00 flying hours.

On June 25, we bombed Toulon harbor in France; specifically, the submarine pens. We had been there before and it was no picnic, plus it was more than 750 miles one way, which meant a long day. When we arrived at Toulon, the weather was so poor that we could not see the target to bomb. We ran into a little flak and it did no damage to us. Two intrepid Fw 190s attacked, but were soon driven off by our P-38 escort. We were ordered to salvo our bombs in the Mediterranean because of the long distances and large fuel loads we were carrying. We flew 08+30 hours on this mission (28).

On June 27, we were sent to Brod, Yugoslavia. Brod was just across the Adriatic, northeast of San Pan and a relatively short mission. The job was to destroy the railroad marshalling yards there. We ran into medium intensity, inaccurate flak. Most of it exploded well below the formation. We did a good job and could see our bombs "right on target," as Ulmer (1944) described. We took off at 0625 and landed back at San Pan at 1215, for a total of 05+50 on mission 29.

At this point in my tour, I found myself becoming a bit neurotic. We had completed more than half of our missions. This was the statistical point that half of the bomber crews never made. We had been very fortunate until now and the odds for continued fortuity became slimmer on each mission. It wasn't so much a desire for self-preservation, but it was more the idea of taking my crew into combat every day against those odds. I was seriously worried I would lose one of them. We were bound together because we shared a common purpose and fate. Shakespeare said it best in his play, Henry V:

We few, we happy few, we band of brothers;
For he to-day that sheds his blood with me
Shall be my brother; be he ne'er so vile.

We hadn't shed any blood together, but that was becoming more and more likely on each mission.

We were in a situation in which it was impossible to become the masters of our own fate. We had to keep flying until we completed our 50 missions, and no matter how much experience we gained or how proficient we became, the law of averages was against us. I kept my own counsel about my increasingly unsettled mind. I received a letter from Mom about this time and she told me she was attending Mass every day and praying for the safe return of Ed and me. Her faith was inspiring and I decided to go see the Catholic Chaplain, Lt.-Col. Father (Fr.) Jim Murphy.

Fr. Murphy had been in the Army for a while and he seemed to be everywhere: in the club drinking, on the flight line before takeoff, and waiting for us when we returned. Many times, I saw him blessing a crew or airplane before missions or administering the Last Rites to wounded or dead crew members as they were pulled from the airplanes on landing. He played football with the enlisted men and cards with the officers. He enjoyed poker and was one of the best players around. A poker game with Nick and Fr. Murphy around the table always drew a crowd. He had credibility with everyone in the unit.

There was an incident during my time in the 376th when Father Murphy was seeing the group off on a mission. He happened to be inside a B-24, ministering to one of the crew, when the signal flare to taxi was given. The airplane began to move and it was too late for him to dismount. Father Murphy ended up an accidental crew member for the entire mission to Genoa.

This "accident" increased his standing even more among the guys. Even non-Catholics went to Fr. Murphy with their problems. It was not unusual to see them attending Mass and receiving Holy Communion among the Catholic guys.

I spoke with Father within the confines of Confession, so no one would think I was on the edge. Father listened and probably had had many similar conversations with other crew members. He spoke easily and his advice was simple. He said, "Give it up. You aren't in control and it is prideful to think you are. God is. Place your faith and trust your fate to Him. Whatever happens will be right."

He said a few other things, including inviting me to talk anytime. Then he gave me some penance, even though I hadn't actually confessed any sins (or did I?) and gave me absolution. I felt like a huge burden had been lifted when emerging from the confessional.

Fr. Murphy was right. I had taken on the entire mental burden for the crew's welfare and it was affecting my ability to function. It certainly would have negatively impacted my performance at some point, if it had not already. I had a new attitude and wanted to share this with my crew.

I decided to set up a crew meeting around a picnic. I gave Harvey some money and asked him to spread it around his sources in maintenance to get some steaks and figure out how we would cook them. I got the rest of the food from Cookie, in exchange for a promise to get all his cooks a ride in the B-24. I said, "Ok, what about you?" He responded, "L-T (using the letters), I wouldn't fly in that thing if they doubled my pay! These young cooks got no sense. They got a safe job with me here in the mess hall and they can't wait to do sumthin' stupid!"

I told the crew of my own anxiousness and described my epiphany when I gave it up. Not all of the crew was Catholic, so I went light on the religion part. Most of the crew shared their similar feelings of anxiety. They didn't realize this was normal and they were waiting for someone else to bring up the elephant in the room. We agreed that talking about it was helpful. I encouraged them to continue talking to someone: myself, the chaplains, the flight surgeon, or anyone else. To my surprise, a few of them already had.

I guess this was as close as I got to combat fatigue, which they now call PTSD. Surprisingly, the treatment hasn't changed: talking to someone who has been there and done that usually helps. Spirits seemed to rise after the picnic and Harvey told me the enlisted crew really appreciated the opportunity to see how the officers were feeling.

On June 30, we were on the mission sheet to bomb the A/D at Zagreb, Yugoslavia. The weather was briefed as marginal at the target area, an accurate report. It had deteriorated to the point where we couldn't bomb by the time we got there. Harvey Ulmer (1944) recorded, "We ran into medium accurate, heavy-caliber flak, but suffered no damage to ship or crew." We logged 07+00 hours on mission 30.

Mission 31 on July 2 was to Budapest, Hungary, to bomb a German A/D and aircraft repair facility. We flew Vivie again and the ground crew was spot-on with the condition of the airplane. Each time we flew Vivie, it was in better condition than the last. I started thinking that my come-to-Jesus meeting had been pretty effective, and then I remembered that the Line Chief's grisly threat was probably what made the difference.

The briefing was at 0530 and was fairly normal except for the anti-aircraft defenses in the target area. They were as formidable as any we had faced. There were 40 gun positions that contained as many as 200 guns. I was getting anxious and remembered what Father had said. I let it go. The weather was expected to be CAVU all the way to Budapest and back. Takeoff time was 0630. Once we formed up over San Pan at 4,000 feet, the lead ship turned northeast and began a 250-fpm climb to 20,000 feet.

In the target area, the flak was as bad as I had ever experienced. It was so thick it looked like you could walk on it. There was a song about flak made up by an unknown airman, sung to the tune of As Time Goes By:

You must remember this,
The flak can't always miss,
Somebody's gotta die,
The odds are always too damned high,
As flak goes by.
It's still the same old story,

The Eighth gets all the glory,
While we're the ones who die.
The odds are always too damned high,
As flak goes by.

I used to hum it as we flew thru the maelstrom of exploding steel. It was a miracle that we sustained minimal damage to our ship or crew. We were in the minority; most of the 376th bombers in formation had multiple holes and damage. Two aircraft were shot down, one immediately behind us in the formation. My crew was so lucky during our 50 missions. We took plenty of flak and "I don't know how we made it through."

Today we had our own problems. The minimal damage we had sustained from the flak caused the bomb release mechanism to fail and damage to the bomb bay doors . We couldn't drop our load on the target. We could not land with live bombs and a defective release mechanism: What if it suddenly started working over friendly territory? The bombs had to be salvoed.

Once clear of the target area and over water, the bombardier, Charlie Freeman, and Harvey donned portable oxygen bottles and descended into the frigid bomb bay, between the bomb racks, and attempted to free them. They approached this very cold and dangerous job as if it were nothing. Such is the makeup of real heroes.

Their inspection revealed that one of the bomb bay doors was only half-open. It took them a half hour to tear off the damaged bomb bay doors and salvo the live bombs. They were on the verge of frostbite and temperature shock when they finally finished. I submitted both for the Silver Star for their heroic action that day. We arrived back at base behind the formation, around 1315 hours. In the Army's wisdom, the awards were downgraded to Bronze Stars, because they were not literally under enemy fire when their heroic act took place, as is required for a Silver Star.

Mission 32 was on July 4, 1944, and was a milk run to bomb the Pitesti railroad bridge in Romania. We saw no fighters and there was zero flak. I was thankful because this was my first time flying flight lead in a box of four bombers. I had other things to concentrate on this day.

When flying the lead ship, the pilot has to be ever cognizant of what he is doing and how it will affect the trailing ships. All maneuvers must be coordinated and very gentle so the formation can follow and maintain the appropriate position. Flying lead was far more tiring than following back in the formation. The mission was 06 + 15 hours and I was exhausted.

Our next mission, on July 5th, was to attack the sub pens in Toulon Harbor. Fuel loading was going to be critical because of the long distances and unfavorable winds. We would be flying into a 30-mph headwind for 750 miles, considerably reducing our speed. I wanted to take on the maximum amount of fuel (3,614 gallons), but the bomb load of 8,000 pounds and all the other things we had to carry would put the airplane prohibitively over its maximum takeoff weight. I had to calculate how much fuel we could carry, less what it would take for starting and taxi.

I did this down to the last gallon and had Frank check my math. My calculation indicated that with 3,050 gallons, we would be able to get off the ground at about 69,000 pounds. I asked my copilot, Fred, to supervise the refueling of the plane, #42, Flame McGoon, a B-24D flying its 70th consecutive mission. It was an honor to be flying this particular airplane. Usually #42 was reserved for crews that had 40 or more missions under their belt.

Named after a character in the Andy Capp comic strip "Lil Abner," this was of those B-24s that wouldn't quit. Staff Sgt. Harden, the crew chief, and his men were magicians to have amassed a record of 70 consecutive combat missions without the airplane having to turn back because of a mechanical malfunction. Before bedding down the evening before, I asked Fred if the refueling had been completed. He said it hadn't because the fueling guys were behind, but that he would go directly to the airplane in the morning, while I was at the briefing, to ensure the fueling had been done correctly.

Takeoff was at 0740. As soon as I got to Flame McGoon, I checked with Mittles about the refueling: He said, "Taken care of, Cap." When he said this, I asked no further questions: big mistake! We began the start procedure and taxied when signaled. The airplane used up most of the runway as expected on takeoff, but we got off with plenty of speed and it was handling fine. The target area was rife with flak: "Accurate and heavy-caliber, no injuries to crew" as Ulmer (1944) described. We saw no fighters. The target looked like it was toast, but only the bomb damage assessment (BDA), flown by recce and analyzed by intel, would reveal the actual damages.

On the way home, the fuel gauges indicated we had used more fuel than I predicted. I asked Fred about the refueling and he said that he had put exactly 2650 gallons in the tanks. This was 400 gallons less than I told him to put in and to get us home safely! I was angry, but more than that, we were in a dangerous situation, flying over water on the return trip, with the nearest safe landing being Nettuno, about 450 miles away.

Frank calculated that we would have just enough fuel to reach Nettuno, with none to spare. It could have been much worse if the flak we encountered had damaged the fuel tanks. I was mad at Mittles, but furious at myself for this screw-up. I knew Fred was lackadaisical and cavalier toward the routine pre-flight tasks. I should have asked very specifically how much fuel he had taken on and I should have double-checked the tanks before taking off. I was the aircraft commander and I was responsible.

Harvey and I figured out how much we could lean the mixture to conserve fuel and we did so. Frank plotted the best course for Nettuno. Maximum endurance power meant we could not keep up with the formation. Those two-plus hours heading for Nettuno, alone, over the Tyrrhenian Sea were the longest of my life.

I directed the crew to be prepared to ditch, which meant getting their life preservers on and the rafts ready for deployment. As noted earlier, the B-24 was known as one of the worst airplanes to ditch because of its ponderous fuselage hanging below the wing. Even if the wings remained intact and provided some flotation, we would all be under water.

All the fuel gauges were reading empty when Nettuno appeared on the horizon. Frank called the tower and declared an emergency. I planned the approach higher than normal to provide for some additional altitude to glide, in case we lost power. About five miles from the runway threshold, the #1 engine quit. Harvey, Fred, and I quickly shut it down and feathered the prop. We were still in decent shape on the approach except for the adverse yaw because of the dead engine.

A mile out we were still high, and I gauged that we had the runway made. I dumped all the flaps and reduced power to slow the airplane and descend quickly so as not to overshoot the landing area. We had one chance; there would be no go-around. As we passed over the runway threshold, I chopped the power on the remaining three engines and we touched down about 1,000 feet down the 4800-foot runway. On the rollout, #3 and #4 quit. It was impossible to taxi the beast with only one engine, so we shut down #2 and had to endure the indignity of being towed to parking ramp.

While we were waiting for the aircraft to be refueled in Nettuno, the crew walked the beaches where the Allied landing had taken place. I remained with Flame McGoon to supervise the refueling. The guys returned in an hour or so with all kinds of souvenirs. We took off as the sun was setting, flew the two hours to San Pan, and landed in the darkness. We flew a total of 09+00 hours on mission 33.

Upon arrival at San Pan, I was summoned to the ops office. The ops officer, Maj. Burtnett, was an intimidating, 6 foot 4 inch, uni-browed giant with a voice to match his stature. He gave me an ass chewing that to this day remains very real. He tore me down until I felt less than worthless, humiliating me with the most profane language I had ever heard. He completed the 10-minute tirade with, "Don't let it happen again, Lieut. Horn or I will have your ass!" And I believed him!

I also had to endure a lot of genial ribbing from the rest of the pilots. I didn't say anything about Fred's mistake to anyone else, but privately told him that he had breached our trust. I made up my mind then that everything would be double-checked. It was the first time a member of the crew really let me down. Anyone could be distracted from the task at hand and it was my job to be the backup.

This was the major leadership lesson for me, learned at no cost in lives and treasure. By the way, old #42, Flame Magoon, made it to its 76th mission when it was lost over Targoviste, Romania. Talk about beating the odds!

As I passed thru Operations, I saw that we were on the mission sheet for the next day, July 6. The mission was to bomb a railroad bridge at Casarsa, in Northern Italy near Trieste. The mission turned out to be an easy one and I was glad of it. Harvey Ulmer had been tapped to fly with a new crew as instructor engineer. We had a replacement from the ground crew, who seemed fine, but who knows what might happen if things got tough? We flew 06 + 30 hours on mission 34.

Our next mission was on July 8, after a day off, to Markersdorf A/D on the outskirts of Vienna. I had Harvey back now, although he had flown on the 7th with another crew. We were assigned to fly as box leader in B flight. I was expecting tough enemy resistance, based on the briefings, but none materialized; no fighters and no flak. I sensed that the Germans were getting weaker and weaker in Italy and were moving assets to France to oppose the Normandy breakout.

Only 25 aircraft were on this mission and two turned back because of maintenance issues. Our #2 engine started to lose oil pressure on the way home and I shut it down and feathered the propeller. With reduced power, we couldn't lead the box and dropped back. Chalk 2 in the box assumed the lead. We were able to keep pretty close to the formation. While flying behind, I witnessed one of the most stomach-turning incidents of my entire combat tour.

D flight had three B-24s flying in a vee. Chalks 2 and 3 had a lapse of attention and collided in midair, causing both airplanes to become uncontrollable, catch fire, and crash. It had been such a surprisingly easy day and then this. I felt nauseated to witness the death of 22 crew members, deaths that only happened because the pilots took their eye off the ball. Others on my crew saw the accident occur and were equally disturbed by it.

We had always discussed and agreed that formation flying involved the entire crew and required everyone's eyes and heads on a swivel. Here we had a ghastly example of what could happen if there was a lapse in our concentration. It did not have to happen, but it did, and a lot of families would be irreparably hurt. We received credit for two missions (35/36) and our flying time was 07+30 hours. San Pan was a sad place that evening, knowing that some of our own would never return because of an entirely preventable accident.

On July 9, we were assigned as B flight leader in the 2nd Section of four bombers flying in a diamond formation. The destination was Ploesti again, where we had learned to expect a lot of enemy opposition. We took off at 0530 with 28 airplanes, and one turned back after takeoff. The route was sort of roundabout to avoid enemy installations.

On this run, Ulmer (1944) wrote, "Ran into accurate, intense, heavy-caliber flak." We received several hits, but no crew member and nothing major on the airplane was damaged. The target was so obscured by smoke that it was hard to tell if we had hit anything. We saw nothing of the Luftwaffe, and our P-51 escorts put on an aerobatics show before they headed home. As I said, we flew a roundabout route and turned a seven-hour flight into nine hours. Extra flying beats getting shot at any day! This was missions 37/38, fully two thirds of the way toward our ticket home.

My crew was overdue for R&R, which usually came about midway thru the 50 missions. We were pulled off the line on July 10 and sent to Capri for a week. Capri is a small island of approximately 6½ square miles, located in the Tyrrhenian Sea off the Sorrentine Peninsula, on the south side of the Gulf of Naples, in the Campania region of Italy.

The main town, Capri, shared the same name as the island. It had been a resort since Roman times. Capri was basically a large, monolithic limestone rock. The sides of the island were perpendicular, its cliffs plunging vertically into the sea. The surface of the island was composed of more cliffs. There were only two small harbors on the island, Marina Piccolo on the south and Marina Grande on the north, both prototypically scenic.

The occupying Americans claimed the island for the Army Air Force R&R center, as soon hostilities moved north. In normal times, Capri was a sleepy tourist destination that was a magnet for artists and had hosted the likes of John Singer Sargent, famous American portrait painter; the German painter August Kopish, who rediscovered the Blue Grotto; Claude Debussy, French composer and conductor; and English writer, William Somerset Maugham. All of these artists incorporated Capri into notable works of their art.

As an R&R center, Capri was a bustling place overrun by GIs taking a well-deserved break from the war. Cars had never been allowed in the city, but during the occupation, many military vehicles were used to shuttle supplies to the many hotels in use by U.S. Forces. Although the majority of the war bypassed Capri as strategically unimportant, the Caprisians were as destitute as the rest of the Italians. They were only too happy to be a part of the economic engine the R&R center brought.

To me, Capri was a beautiful, romantic place that I could only have dreamed of, growing up in Newburgh. It made me think of Eleanore and how much she would have loved the place. I promised myself that we would come back together.

Frank and I were married men and we decided to try to avoid the typical R&R hangouts such as bars, dance halls, and the like. Even as small as Capri was, it wasn't difficult to get away from the hustle and bustle. We took excursions, mostly on foot, to every corner of the island and it was exhausting. I hadn't had much physical activity since coming to Italy, and hiking from the beach to Capri city was a short but wicked steep hike.

We saw the natural beauty of the island with its Roman ruins, went swimming in the beautiful blue water, and ate and drank wonderful food. And for five days, we slept peacefully, on clean sheets, with stomachs full of great food. It was incredibly relaxing to unwind from the pace of flying missions and to experience the life amenities that were absent in San Pan. The only thing missing was my beautiful Eleanore. I felt guilty that she could not share this experience with me.

As Chaucer said, "All good things must come to an end." After five glorious days, we took the ferry to Naples and picked up a B-24 to fly home to San Pan.

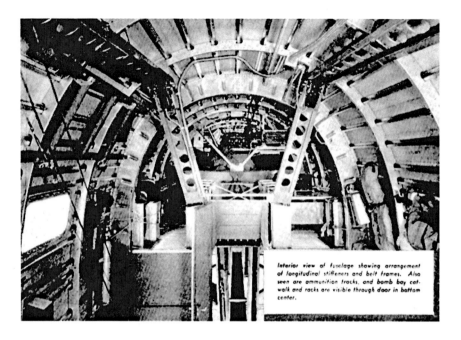

Interior view of fuselage showing arrangement of longitudinal stiffeners and belt frames. Also seen are ammunition tracks, and bomb bay catwalk and racks are visible through door in bottom center.

The interior of the B-24, seen from behind the pilot's station looking rearward. Note the narrow walkway in the center between the bomb racks.

USAAF via author.

The 515th Squadron mess hall with tables and chairs made from the wood scrounged from ammo crates.

Donald Johnstone via author.

B-24D "Flame McGoon."
Lt. William J. Paterick via author.

Chapter 5

The Home Stretch

WE returned from R&R to San Pan on July 22. The contrast between the stress-free, clean, inviting environment at Capri and the dusty bleakness of our base could not have been starker. In the time it took for us to walk from the flight line to our tents, our clean uniforms were coated in a thin layer of dust. Coming back to our existence in San Pan was difficult. I salved myself with the thought that we were 70 percent through the magic 50-mission ticket home. I hadn't flown in more than a week (it felt like a month), but got busy arranging an airplane to fly the next day to hone our crew's flying skills.

Harvey and I had a crew meeting that evening to make sure everyone was focused on business again. All the guys were anxious to share their Capri R&R stories. Some were pretty typical of G.I.s on leave—their R&R consisted of lots of I & I (intoxication and intercourse)!

Harvey did most of the talking and cleverly used a baseball metaphor to get the guys focused: "Our crew is like a baseball team in the seventh inning of a close game. We are protecting a small lead, and if we want to win, we have to keep our heads in the game." Harvey was such an incredible leader; the little talk was very effective.

It was my turn, and Harvey turned the meeting over to me. He had pretty much said all that was necessary so I simply endorsed what he said and asked the guys to think about how wonderful it was going to be to get home. I asked them to consider what we would need to do as a crew to make our homecoming a reality: work together, fly safely, keep our heads on a swivel, and take care of our airplanes and equipment.

Harvey told the enlisted guys to lay out all their flight gear right after the meeting to ensure it was mission-ready. He had already made arrangements with the crew chief to go over Sad Sack, the B-24H we would use for practice flying. The enlisted guys went for their equipment checks and we officers talked a bit more and drifted off to prepare for our training flight.

The training flight on the 23rd went pretty well. The excitement of the R&R had not quite worn off and it took an hour or so to get everyone focused. We had clearance to test fire all the guns and flew south off the coast near Porto Cesareo, where a few small, uninhabited islands were designated as a firing range. The guys got busy with the machine guns. I let Fred vacate the co-pilot's seat to have a go as a waist gunner. Harvey moved up to Fred's seat and I gave him some flying lessons; he was a natural. To be sure, I was within inches of the controls while he tried his hand at the four-engined B-24, not exactly a primary trainer.

The mission for July 24 came down shortly after we returned from our training flight in the late afternoon. It was to bomb the harbor in Genoa again. The route was to cross the peninsula to Nettuno and then parallel the western coast over water until turning north-northeast toward Genoa on the bomb run. The return had us turning left over the target, making a wide left arc until over the Mediterranean, and retracing our inbound route.

Flying to Genoa had never been much of a problem except for the large amounts of fuel needed for the nine-hour trip. This seemed to be a good mission to ease back into the war after R&R. It turned out the mission was not as easy as anticipated. We ran into accurate, medium-caliber flak. We suffered no damages or injuries to the crew, but the flight nevertheless provided us some anxious and exciting moments. No ships were lost on mission 39.

After a day off on July 26, the group was assigned the task to attack the Markerdorf A/D near Graz, Austria where Me 109s were manufactured. Recce had also detected numerous Me 109s dispersed on the three airfields in the target area. Four bomber wings were going on this mission and the 47th Wing was assigned to attack the Tullan A/D, 65 miles west of Vienna. Take-off time was 0730, which meant an early wake-up call. As I walked to the mess hall, I marveled at how nice the weather actually was at San Pan. The disc of the sun rose reddish and cool. It was so pleasant, I took my powdered eggs and bread outside to enjoy the sunrise.

After breakfast, the crew drifted off to our respective briefing rooms to see what was in store for us on mission 40. This was a serious target that was expected to be defended by 200 or more fighter aircraft, beginning 30-45 minutes before the target area. The S-2 (intelligence staff officer) told us flak was briefed as "nonc" in the target area, based on the recce flight. This nugget of non-intelligence evoked peals of laughter and derision from the pilots in the briefing room. We all knew that simply because the recce plane didn't get shot at, didn't mean the guns were not there. The S-2, slightly embarrassed, quickly introduced the weather officer and slinked off the stage as fast as he could.

We were assigned to be the box leader in B flight of the 2nd Section. Takeoff was normal and the bombers formed up and we began a climb to 20,000 feet. After an hour of flying, our formation of 27 B-24s was formed and we headed north across the Adriatic for Austria. The weather was fine until we crossed the Alps at 25,000 feet, when the clouds obscured the ground from there to the target. The lead ship of our 376th formation was a Pathfinder, a bomber with new radar that could direct the formation over the target with reasonable accuracy.

Dropping bombs with a Pathfinder ship was a timing exercise. Frank quickly calculated when we would be over the target, based on when the lead ship dropped its bombs. He said, "Two minutes and eight seconds after the Pathfinder drops, we should drop."

I set my countdown timer and when the time elapsed, I said "mark", Charlie pushed the pickle button to release the bombs and responded with "bombs away". Our bomber rose immediately and felt more responsive after discharging three tons of bombs. We received very little flak over the target, primarily because of the overcast skies, and we saw no fighters outside the target area.

This was the first time our unit had employed a Pathfinder aircraft and I liked it. It enabled us to do our job when weather over the target was lousy and it gave another level of safety to defend against flak. The only downside was that we had no idea how effective our bombs were. That did not worry us; BDA was someone else's job! The flight back to San Pan was uneventful and we logged 07+30 hours.

By this time in 1944, Major General Nathan Twining, the 15th Air Force commander, had built the unit up to its maximum strength of approximately 900 bombers and 1,100 crews to fly them. Our operational tempo was reduced because there were more bombers and crews available to attack fewer and fewer targets. I flew twice as much in the first half of my tour as in the second half. This made it easier on the crews as well as on the airplanes. It also meant that we would be overseas longer to get to the magic 50.

Another rumor that was circulating was that because the German fighter strength had been depleted so much, two-credit missions might be eliminated. Turned out that was just a rumor, but it was a morale buster until the truth was sorted out. My experience over 50 missions was that on a given day, the Luftwaffe could generate a massive fighter attack around a target area if they choose to. It was just luck if they went after someone else and you were spared.

After the July 26 mission, we had a couple of days where we relaxed and did not do much of anything. Had we had an assigned aircraft, the time could have been used more productively.

Summer in southern Italy is hot and dusty. The few bodies of fresh water were incubators for malarial mosquitoes. Of course, the Army had a malaria prevention program that included mosquito control, sleeping under mosquito netting, and anti-malarial drugs. Everyone in the 15th Air Force was required to take a daily Atabrine tablet to prevent malaria. Atabrine had a lot of different side effects. One common side effect was that it gave a yellowish cast to our skin, which was pretty harmless. Another was diarrhea, which could be mighty uncomfortable at 20,000 feet.

Some of the other side effects were nausea and headaches. Many GIs resisted taking the drugs because of specious rumors that they caused impotence and sterility. Because of the rumors,

Atabrine was not very popular with the GIs and dodges to avoid taking the medication were legendary. One enlisted man switched the Atabrine labels in the pharmacy, and for weeks, the entire group was taking another medication that looked like Atabrine. The flight surgeon finally got wise because everyone's yellow tint was gone. We never did find out what we had actually taken.

Of course, spitting the pill out was another less complicated way to avoid it and it was common to see discarded tablets on the ground. The aircraft commander was responsible for ensuring that his crew took the tablets. I took the responsibility pretty seriously because malaria, once contracted, could have lifelong health effects. Also, malaria was a grounding condition and we would have to replace any afflicted crew member. Accepting a replacement this close to the goal of 50 missions was considered extremely bad juju. I checked that the officers complied and Harvey checked the enlisted crewmen daily. We never had any problems that I was aware of.

The following day's mission came down during supper on July 29 and immediately made it to the grapevine in the mess hall. The 376th was tasked to lead more than three-plus bomber wings on the following day's mission, the location of which would be revealed during the mission briefing the next day.

Our assigned ship, #96, Diddlin' Dolly II, was an older D model and would be flying on the right wing of the flight leader of the entire mission (first section of A flight). This was the backup lead position. If anything happened to the flight lead ship, it would be our job to take over and lead the mission of 400-plus bombers. Diddlin' Dolly II had a reputation for being a bit short on power, but otherwise reliable.

It was common to put the weakest airplanes up front in formations, so those following would have no problem keeping up. I had never been this close to being a mission leader and was unsettled about it. I prayed hard that nothing would happen to the flight lead. Harvey and the ground crew chief were up until all hours, going over the airplane. Since we might end up as the flight lead, Frank and I discussed the criticality of his navigation.

Of course, we would not know the destination of the mission destination until the mission briefing in the morning.

We had a 0645 takeoff and got up two hours prior. First, I asked Fred and Charlie to get out to the ship with Harvey as soon as possible and give her another once-over while I went to the mission briefing an hour and a half before takeoff. The target was a refinery complex near Budapest consisting of Blechhammer North and Blechhammer South, each a little more than a square mile wide, with about two miles separating them. The refinery was converting bituminous coal into various gasoline fuels, including high-octane aviation gas.

Like many of Germany's war industries, the refinery was operated largely by slave labor supervised by the SS. Slave labor camps dotted the area. Attacking enemy facilities where slave labor was known to be, always concerned me. Destroying the Nazi war-making capability was the accepted strategy to end the war. The deaths that were sure to occur—of those working there against their will—gave me pause about the morality of the strategy. In the end, I reasoned there was no intent to kill the slave workers, but their deaths were an unintended consequence of the moral action to end the war. And I lived with that.

Intel briefed that there that were only two known flak guns in the refinery area. Enemy fighters were not expected because most of them had been shifted to other locations. Light enemy resistance? We all knew better and took the information with a grain of salt.

Budapest was a three to four-hour flight from San Pan, so fuel wasn't a problem. The route took us due north to the Yugoslavian coast, then northeast to the target. Following the bomb run, we were to break left off the target, head west to Croatia, and then south to home base. Our bomb load consisted of 12, 500-pound bombs. Some of the aircraft following carried incendiary bombs.

Diddlin' Dolly II performed borderline on takeoff at 0700. She could barely make the prescribed 44 MAP (manifold pressure) on the #2 and #3 engines for takeoff. We used the better part of 4,500 feet to get aloft. Once in the air, it flew OK:

straight, in trim, and without overheating. The multi-Wing size of the mission demanded more time getting formed up, but by 0800, we were in formation over Cartelluccio, Italy, where the 49th Bomber Wing was stationed. We headed north for the target.

This mission ran very smoothly; nothing happened to the flight lead and we ran into no opposition from flak or fighters. The weather was good over the target and we were accurate with our bombs. After dropping the ordnance, we made a gradual left turn to the west, where we could see the subsequent waves of bombers coming in behind us. The target looked to be pretty well destroyed. Smoke and fire over our target area prevented any precise assessment of the raid. Nine K-22 cameras took pictures of the target area and they later revealed good results. We flew a total of 06+30 hours on the mission.

The crew and I were enjoying a bit of a time off because of the increase in bomber crews. Harvey, however, was a check engineer, and in the interim, he was tasked to fly with 2nd Lieut. Al Hoover's crew in Send Me Baby to check out a new flight engineer. The mission was expected to be an easy one—and it was—with one exception: Send Me Baby took a piece of shrapnel through the floor between the two pilots. Not a second before, Harvey was standing there. In his log, he wrote, "I moved just in time to have it miss me" (Ulmer, 1944). By this time in our tour, we were all getting a little superstitious and Harvey begged me to protect him from having to fly with other crews. I think this was the last time he did.

When our next mission, 41, came down on August 9, it took us back to Budapest to bomb the Vecses A/D. This was to be another multi-wing mission with our group, the 47th Bomb Wing, leading the 49th and 55th Bomb Wings. Within the 47th, the 376th was again tasked to lead the attack. Our airplane was #59, a squawk-free B-24H. We were the box leader of B flight, directly behind the flight leader's vee. This time, we had a P-38 fighter escort. It was briefed that there were up to 130 flak guns around the target area, but we did not see any flak or fighters. It was a milk run. We flew 06+00 hours on the mission and were back at San Pan by 1330.

The 376th was tasked to participate in a maximum effort to Ploesti on August 10. My crew was not on the flight schedule, which turned out to be a blessing, lucky and fortuitous. Six out of the 27 bombers on the mission were shot down by enemy flak and fighters. A few more were severely damaged and had to limp home. This was the worst day for the 376th during my time overseas. [Author's note: Coincidentally, on August 10, 1970, my unit in Vietnam experienced its worst losses during my tour. Mercifully I was spared.]

Three bombers were lost to heavy, accurate flak over the target, but the real action started when the formation made a descending left turn after clearing the target area. The flight reformed after emerging from the intense black cloud of flak, only to be met by a formations of enemy fighters. From the stories of those present, there must have been 60 Me 109s and Fw 190s that attacked our formation.

This was a real gunfight: an amazing, confusing, fierce air battle between the German fighters and our escorting P-51s, supported by the machine guns in our bombers. The attacks were very aggressive, with enemy fighters closing within 50 to 100 yards of the formation. They fired machine guns, 20mm cannons, and rockets. There were no head-on attacks this time, but the enemy fighters made their attacks singly, in pairs, in fours, and eight fighters abreast. Some dove away low after making their passes, while others zoomed upwards.

Many fighters exposed their bellies as they finished their passes, making good targets for our gunners. These mistakes were costly for the Luftwaffe and were the result of inexperienced pilots. Most of the experienced Luftwaffe pilots had already been killed or captured and Germany was forced to reduce the length and quality of fighter pilot training.

Some of our crews reported seeing our own gunners, in the excitement of the brawl, hitting our P-51 escorts as they were in pursuit of the enemy fighters. Mustangs could be mistaken for Me 109s from a distance, except for the scoop on the P-51's belly.

When P-51s were far enough away so that the American flag painted on the P-51's fuselage couldn't be readily seen, or when they were banking so their belly scoops couldn't be seen, it was difficult for our gunners to tell them apart. Such was the fog of battle in air combat.

Our formation was flying so tight that empty shell casings were hitting the airplanes following in the formation, causing significant damage to otherwise unmolested bombers. Holes in the leading edges of wings and other less critical sheet metal areas kept the ground crews busy for weeks.

The 376th gunners acquitted themselves extremely well, accounting for shooting down 26 fighters, getting eight more probables, and damaging four more. Clendinen (2010), who participated in the battle, wrote, "The flak was the heaviest I have ever seen! God was with us all the way! As a result of the gigantic air battle, six of our group's bombers were shot down by enemy fighters." Thirteen more were damaged from flak and fighters.

Sixty-one of our group's airmen were missing in action, one ball turret gunner was killed, and four crew members were severely wounded. Capps (1997) reported, "The sky was filled with 10 to 20 parachutes much of the time during the air battle." One squadron lost six of the eight bombers it sent on the mission.

The air battle on August 10 did not end the 376th's flirtation with danger. After the enemy fighters ran out of fuel and left, the formation ran into heavy and accurate flak on the way back from the target area. Through a navigation error by the flight lead, the formation flew over Sarajevo. The flak there put more holes in the bombers. This probably would not have happened had my crew, specifically Frank Belasco, been on the mission, using his coded system to keep the flight lead navigator on course. I felt a little guilty about that aspect of the mission, but overall, I was very grateful we missed this one. The battered Liberandos arrived at San Pan at 1250 hours and had logged 06 + 25 hours of flight time.

To set the stage for our mid-August missions, it's necessary to be aware of the overall allied strategy. Operation Dragoon was the Allied invasion of southern France on August 15, 1944.

As in Normandy, the invasion was initiated with an airborne assault by the 1st Airborne Task Force, followed by an amphibious assault by the 6th Army Group, consisting of the American 7th Army followed by elements of the French 1st Army. The landing caused the German Army Group G to abandon southern France and retreat under constant Allied attacks to the Vosges Mountains, where some of the least known, but most vicious combat of the war occurred (Bonn, 2006).

Despite being a large and complex amphibious operation, Operation Dragoon was well executed and the results were never in doubt. Operation Dragoon was overshadowed by the larger Operation Overlord in Normandy (D-Day) two months earlier, where the outcome of that operation was in doubt for several days.

At the time, we weren't aware of Operation Dragoon, but the next few days' missions were in support of it. The missions for August 12 came down before chow, the night before. We were only told to plan for maximum range and that we would be carrying a mix of 1,000- and 2,000-pound, bunker-busting bombs.

At the next morning's briefing, we found out the target destination was the Marseille coastal defenses. Because of the distances involved, and ever mindful of our earlier experiences, Frank and I calculated the fuel load very carefully, and Fred as well as Frank supervised the refueling to ensure we had no SNAFUs. I double-checked the fuel load before climbing in the airplane. This was to be a 10-hour mission, taking us across the Italian peninsula toward Anzio, going feet wet there and over the southern tip of Corsica to a point south of Marseille, where we would turn northwest for the bomb run. We would break left over the target and follow a wide arc back over the sea to get home.

It was a torrid day in San Pan, around 90 degrees, and the airplanes would be heavy because of the full bomb load and extra fuel need for the mission. Our assigned airplane was # 41, Bad Benny, a decent B-24G. After loading her with three 2,000-pound bombs and almost 20,000 pounds (3,300 gallons) of fuel, Bad

Benny was overweight at north of 69,000 pounds. The heavy airplane, coupled with the high-density altitude because of the heat, elevated the normal takeoff pucker factor to sphincter-strangling levels!

We were in the second section and would be among the first to start and take off. Normally that would be a good thing. Today it didn't allow us any time to burn off fuel while waiting in line to take off. At the appropriate time in the checklist, Harvey started the APU, which was basically a single-cylinder lawn mower engine. We called it "Putt-Putt." Putt-Putt powered a generator to boost the battery when starting the first engine, usually #3.

Once #3 was started, it had its own generators to assist in starting the other engines and Putt-Putt was shut down. I took my time during the engine run-up to burn as much fuel as possible and to check each engine's operation: oil pressure, RPM, magnetos, propellers, back-up systems, and so on. Finally, before taxiing, I called out the pre-takeoff checklist and Fred responded:

"Flaps"

"Half"

"Trim"

"Set for takeoff"

After Fred set the trim, I added a little extra nose up adjustment to compensate for our extreme weight. This would make it easier to raise the nose for rotation.

"Boost pumps"

"On"

"Mixture"

"Auto-rich"

"Props"

"Full RPM"

"Superchargers"

"Set"

And so on, until I asked for a response from each crew member over the intercom, indicating whether he was ready for takeoff. Ed Seibert, our young rear gunner, responded with, "I was born ready, Cap," adding a little humor. I couldn't appreciate it though anticipating the dangerous takeoff before us.

A white flare from the control tower was the signal to begin taxiing in turn to the runway. As the heavily laden B-24s lumbered across the uneven taxiways and multiple surfaces, they rocked and dipped, looking like a line of drunken hippos.

When our turn came, I lined up the big bomber on the runway, set the brakes, and throttled up the four 1,200-horsepower Pratt & Whitney engines until they were at max power and literally roaring to be loosed. We checked that each engine was making 44 inches of MAP and 2,700 RPM. I gave the airplane in front of me 30 seconds from beginning his takeoff roll until I released the brakes. We lurched forward on the roll, vibrating and roaring to a deafening decibel level. Acceleration was slow because of our weight.

Fred's eyes were glued to the airspeed indicator as he called off each increase of 10 miles per hour. Mine were fixed down the runway. We needed 60 mph of airspeed before rotating the nose and 105 mph to lift off. Our preflight calculations indicated we would have to attain 105 mph at or before reaching 3,000 feet of the 5,000-foot runway. If we didn't reach that speed, I would have adequate remaining runway to stop the bomber if we had to abort the takeoff.

Fred called 60 mph, 70 mph, after using 2,000 feet of the runway. At 60, I pulled gently on the controls and the nose lifted skyward. My view of the runway ahead vanished and I used my peripheral vision to keep us lined up. We were pointed skyward, but the main gear was still rolling along the runway. Benny strained under the weight and power, moving to 80 mph, 90 mph.

The fiery loss of #93 on takeoff with Allen Bunker aboard flashed through my mind. The 3,000-foot marker was coming at us like a train. At the 3,000-foot marker, Fred had not called 100. I reached for the throttles to abort the takeoff at maybe 3,100 feet. As my hand was going forward, he called 100. I withdrew my right hand back to the control wheel and gave a gentle pull, but nothing happened!

By this time, we had consumed 3,500 feet of runway. At 110 mph and another 500 feet of runway gobbled up, it was too late to safely abort. I said a silent prayer and finally Benny flew herself off the ground. We were flying, but barely, and we needed more speed to establish a safe climb. I snapped to Fred, "Gear up," to remove that drag from the airstream. I tapped the brakes to stop the wheels from turning as they retracted. The B-24 landing gear retraction mechanism was reasonably reliable. My theory was its reliability was a function of its slow operating speed. It operated so slowly, it never created enough friction to wear out any parts. With the landing gear tucked away, we began to gain speed.

We were already five miles away from San Pan at olive treetop level, and had probably caused untold surprise to both humans and animals we had overflown. Upon reaching our climb speed of 160 mph, we started a 250-fpm rate of climb and began a gradual retraction of the flaps, so as not to cause the airplane to settle as it lost the additional lift from the flaps. Only then did I back the throttles off to climb power, 40 inches.

My palms were sweaty and I had a death grip on the control wheel, but I could relax a bit now. Definitely, that was the most perilous takeoff I ever made. When an airplane is commanded to exceed its limitations and it is beyond the point of no return, all the pilot can do is be gentle on the controls and wait for her to respond, or not! It is a feeling of utter helplessness and an excellent moment for prayer.

As we climbed and experienced the temperature lapse rate, we were refreshed by the cooler air. We would be flying at 20,000 feet, where the temperature would be a chilly 20 degrees. In the winter months, combat aircrews experienced temperatures as low as 40 or 50 degrees below 0 at mission altitudes. Today, after the heat at San Pan and the sweat-inducing takeoff, the cool air was especially welcome. Two airplanes returned early because of maintenance issues.

We had a P-38 escort into the target area, but didn't need it as the Luftwaffe was absent. Our bombs were from 20,000 feet and Charlie said that our accuracy looked good. Moderate flak defended the target and several aircraft were hit, but none lost. Bad Benny suffered no damage on this 9-hour mission. Other than the takeoff, it went smoothly. We took off at 0700 and landed at 1600. It was a long day!

We were on the schedule to fly again on August 13 to bomb the gun positions around the harbor in Toulon, France. This was another long mission that would require almost full fuel. We drew Bad Benny again, which was a good thing. We knew the aircraft. The temperature had moderated a bit and the bomb load for this trip was only 10 500-pound bombs. We would be almost a thousand pounds lighter, so the pucker factor on takeoff from San Pan would not be quite as bad the previous day.

As anticipated, the takeoff was almost routine. The slightly cooler weather and light bomb load made all the difference. We took off at 0915 and landed at 1700.

Our Wing was split for the attack: half would bomb the marshalling yards around Avignon, which were supporting the submarines in Toulon to the southwest, and half would bomb gun emplacements on small islands in the harbor. We drew the latter mission and pasted the small islands. Today, we had no flak or fighters and the mission went smoothly.

Although my crew was not on the schedule, the 376th flew additional missions on August 14 and 15 in support of Dragoon. On August 15, the 376th participated in the preparation of the landing beaches in the vicinity of St. Tropez. The possibility of enemy fighters in the landing area was briefed as being low. Also, U.S. Navy carrier aircraft would be in the landing area.

To avoid the possibility of friendly fire mistakes, our gunners were prohibited from firing, even test firing their machine guns. The crews weren't happy about this restriction. As it turned out, the Germans were not foolish enough to launch fighters against the overwhelming task force. However, there was flak and the 376th lost one bomber on that day.

With the landing in southern France a success, the 15th Air Force turned its attention back toward a familiar target for a final push to, once and for all, destroy it. Rumor had it that it would be Ploesti. It turned out the mission on August 17 was mission 44 for us and was over Ploesti. My dread of returning there prompted me to have a crew meeting after supper the night before. We were so close to completing our 50 missions, I didn't want anything to happen now. The crew was very confident and cool about the task, which reassured me. We were assigned bomber #59, Pretty Baby, an airplane we had never flown. Harvey organized the extra preparations we would take to ensure its readiness.

After breakfast, Fred and I went to the pilots' briefing and were told of increased flak fortifications around Ploesti. It was hard to believe the Germans could have installed more! Expected enemy fighter resistance was briefed to be low. The flak situation didn't inspire confidence, however, and we anticipated a rough ride.

We had a 0615 takeoff time, which meant an early morning. Four bomber groups were to be involved. The 376th would be the second group over the target, so the 239 flak guns would have established the range of the formations and would have plenty of ammo left when we arrived over the target. Our specific target was a railroad facility associated with the oil refinery.

Takeoff was into a beautiful, clear morning at San Pan. The route took us directly east over the Adriatic across Yugoslavia and Bulgaria to Ploesti. After the bombing run, we were to break north and return via the same route. The weather was severe clear all the way to the target. Our fighter escort, the 332nd Red Tails in their new P-51s, picked us up as we crossed into Yugoslavia. About a hundred miles from the target, the formation was viciously attacked by dozens of Me 109s, but only a few actually broke through our 332nd fighter escort. The objective of the German fighters was to strip the bombers of the fighter coverage and destroy or otherwise prevent the bombers from delivering their ordinance.

The Luftwaffe devised all sorts of ways to lure the fighters away from the bombers to do so. The best escorts, like the 332nd, doggedly refused to leave the bomber formations. The Red Tails had successfully fended off the 109 attack when a second wave of Fw 190s came in behind them. Several of the 190s tore right through the formation, machine guns blasting. "They were so close I could look the German fighter pilots in the eye as they passed." It was a gunfight of gut-wrenching violence, brutality, and mayhem of the first order. I was terrified but managed to hold it together.

There were so many German fighters that our escort began to break away from the bomber formation in pairs to go after them. The melee that followed around the bomber formations was incredible. They ranged out of sight both above and below us. The multi-dimensional aspect of air-to-air-combat makes it a point-and-shoot affair of the highest order. The pointing part was the most difficult part of the equation, lining up a shot on the enemy while avoiding his ability to line up on you. I really admired the flying skill of the fighter jocks and was eternally grateful for their support.

Half a dozen enemy fighters bought the farm, but I was focused on my flying and unable to pay much attention. Ultimately, there were probably more fighter losses, but no bombers in our formation were lost. As we closed in on the Ploesti target, the enemy fighters and our escort backed off and the flak commenced.

Ploesti was murderous this day. It required every ounce of my concentration to hold my position in the formation and avoid the aircraft around me. There was a lot of flinching and terror-induced movement within the formation. The crew was keeping me clear of other aircraft and the volume of their advice over the intercom was directly related to the proximity of other aircraft.

As we approached Ploesti, the clear skies gave way to a target area hidden by smoke, clouds, and fog. Finally, it was time to turn the airplane over to the bombardier for the final bomb run. Charlie called, "I got the airplane, Cap." I responded, "You got the airplane."

Our flight leader advised the target was too obscured to bomb, so we didn't. I took control back from Charlie and followed the leader out of the target area. The flak continued unabated and we were jostled around something fierce. All told on this day, Ulmer (1944) recorded we were in the flak for 12-15 minutes. It seemed longer.

We were in the first box of the second section of the formation. D flight of the first section was immediately in front of us. Two bombers in that section, flown by 2nd Lieut. H.V. Ford and 2nd Lieut. J.R. McConnaughey, were hit and disintegrated before our eyes. We literally flew through pieces of the two planes and crews. We heard the calls over the radio for all crew members to look for parachutes. Back at base, the intel debriefers would compare what all the crew members saw and try to figure out how many of the crew escaped the dying aircraft and where they might have landed.

The formation was making a gradual turn northward out of the target area, all the while enduring the lethal flak barrage. I remember thinking, "I can't wait to get out of here and back to the Luftwaffe." We had taken a number of shrapnel hits to this point, but nothing debilitating. All four engines were still running and we weren't leaking any fuel or vital fluids.

Presently, our return fighter escort appeared—and none too soon—as a flock of Luftwaffe fighters were reported coming out of the sun to our rear. This time, we had P-38s from the 82nd Fighter Group out of Lesina, Italy, and they did their job effectively. Once we went feet wet over the Adriatic, we discovered that the 376th had lost an additional bomber flown by 2nd Lieut. M.K. Westby, to flak over the target. Three bombers out of the 25 that made it to the target were lost. That was more than what was considered as a sustainable (10 percent) loss rate and no bombs were dropped on the target! The war wasn't getting any easier. Harvey also discovered a significant hydraulic leak in our ship that insured we would have to hand crank the landing gear down. We landed at a grim San Pan around 1400 after flying 06+45.

A funny thing happened as I was walking to the 6x6 truck for my ride to debriefing and thinking of my two ounces of whiskey. One of the Black soldiers from the security group approached me and saluted. He asked, "Suh, how did them Red Tails treat you today?" I stopped in my tracks and thought,

"How could he know who our fighter escort was?" I said, "Well, trooper, I can't say who the escort was, but it was tough out there today and the fact that we are here testifies to the great job they did." I asked him how he had come upon that information about the Red Tails. He said with a conspiratorial grin and wink, "Suh, we get around," saluted, and walked off.

In debriefing, we found out that it appeared as if 30 chutes were counted exiting the downed aircraft and we were thankful for that. I was sad that the guys would end up sitting out the war in a Luftwaffe POW camp, but happy that the shooting part of the war was over for them.

After debriefing, I went back out to our airplane with Harvey and Frank to count the holes in it. There was a total of 30 from machine guns (clean round holes) and flak (jagged, irregular holes), some large enough to put your fist through. I said to the guys, "We cheated death again." I thought to myself, "How much more Divine security or luck do we rate?" We did not know it at the time, but this was our last trip to Ploesti. We received credit for two missions, 44 and 45. The 15th Air Force's battle of Ploesti went on for another five days.

Our next mission, on August 22, was to Lobau, near Vienna, another heavily defended oil storage facility. More than 300 Luftwaffe fighters were in the area, as well as in excess of 330 heavy flak guns. Now that Ploesti was in ashes, the remaining oil facilities became that much more valuable to the Germans. We were assigned bomber # 41, Bad Benny, which had proven to be a reliable ride.

In addition to the Lobau facility, there were to be coordinating simultaneous attacks all around Vienna, particularly on the A/Ds to suppress fighter defense. This meant lots of air traffic in the area, all going in different directions. All told, 400-500 bombers would be in the area. There would also be fighter escort and protection around the target.

This mission had all the earmarks of danger from the standpoint of congestion alone. We took off at 0530 into a beautiful early morning sky. As soon as we lifted off from San Pan, we saw the sun rising above the Adriatic. It was an idyllic beginning to another day of doing the devil's work with our instruments of death and destruction.

I seldom had any time to think about the moral aspects of the war and never had to ponder the deliberate bombing of non-combatant civilians, as the Eighth Air Force did when they fire-bombed Hamburg and Dresden. Other than the previously dis-cussed dilemma of slave labor and the destruction of icons of Western civilization, our missions were ethically unambiguous. The 15th Air Force went after military targets. If non-combatants were hit, it was incidental to the military objective.

The trip to the target was easy. No enemy fighters met us. Once inside the Vienna defensive perimeter, we were fiercely attacked by intense and heavy-caliber flak. I could hear the skin of our ship being ripped as she absorbed the shrapnel, but all the mechanical bits continued to function and we pushed on. I heard several Mayday calls from ships in the rear of the formation.

As we approached the target on the bomb run, I turned the airplane over to Charlie and gazed at the beautiful skyline of Vienna in the distance amidst the much closer lethal black puffs of flak. It was a stark contrast between what men were capable of constructing—inspiring architecture and destruction employing horrific weapons. The bomb run complete, we broke to the right to exit the target area.

Many ships in the formation had been hit, had lost one or more engines, and were limping home. The flight lead throttled back to 140 mph so that some of the stragglers could keep up. Otherwise, he might have been leading a flight of one by the time he got to San Pan. In the end, three ships were shot down over the target, two ditched in the Adriatic, and those crews were immediately rescued. Ten more ships received serious flak damage, including us. We flew 07+30 on the mission and got credit for two missions, 47 and 48.

The 15th Air Force continued to pound the Ploesti target until August 23, 1944, when the campaign came to an end. On August 23, Romania bowed to the inevitable, breaking its en-forced alliance with Germany and siding with the Allies. The four-month-long campaign had seen the launch of 5,675 bombing sorties, including one where the bombers were P-38s. The bombers had dropped 14,000 tons of ordnance on the refinery complex at a cost of 282 U.S. and 38 British aircraft and 3,200 Allied lives.

The 376th Bomb Group lost nine bombers and their crews during August. Additionally, another six airmen were killed and 20-plus wounded on aircraft that were able to return to their base.

The battle for Ploesti eventually proved that persistent strikes could ruin a major industrial complex. In the end, Ploesti's burned and battered refineries were producing just a dribble: a 90 percent reduction in petroleum intended for the Wehrmacht. High-ranking German prisoners told Allied interrogators that the Allies' overall strategic bombing campaign would have been more effective in ending the war if destruction of the German oil facilities had been pursued earlier.

One of the high points for the 376th and all 15th Air Force airmen in August was a sideline drama that played out in the Ploesti region, thanks to the noted Romanian ace, Capt. Constantin Cantacuzino. At war's end, he was credited with 47 victories, flying against the Soviets and Americans, and following Romania's surrender, against the Germans.

In late August, he cooperated with the senior American POW in an effort to prevent Allied airmen from being moved by the Germans or "rescued" by the Soviets. The senior American, Lt.-Col. Gunn, who had been shot down during the August 17 mission, was being held in Bucharest. He wedged himself into an Me 109 with Capt. Cantacuzino and the unlikely duo flew to Italy. The intrepid Romanian then offered to lead rescue aircraft to a field near Bucharest to rescue the POWs.

Capt. Cantacuzino got a quick checkout in a P-51B and led 38 B-17s to the field, enabling 1,161 air crewmen to be returned to safety in Italy (Tillman, 2014). This was a fitting end to the protracted violent drama of Ploesti and answered a lot of prayers. It was a genuine, feel-good moment for the entire 15th Air Force.

Our next mission, on August 27, was to be a first: my crew was chosen to lead 28 bombers from the 376th. Leading the group into air combat was usually the province of the unit's senior officers, commanders, ops officer, etc. It wasn't unheard of, but it was unusual for a 2nd Lieut. pilot to be selected as the mission commander/flight leader. Everyone coveted the flight leader job and many actively lobbied for it. That wasn't my style. I vowed early not be too eager and to never volunteer. I did my job and took care of my crew safely.

It was a rewarding surprise when the John Horn crew was selected, and I knew we could do a good job of it. Harvey was the best engineer in the squadron and Frank was the best navigator in the entire wing, maybe in the whole 15th Air Force. The rest of us were seasoned and well trained.

Maj. Burtnett, the ops officer, called me in after chow and briefed that the mission was to destroy the Avisio railroad viaduct and the time that the 376th was to be on target. This was the same ops officer who chewed my butt after we ran out of fuel in July. Three other bomb groups were participating in this mission, so the timing and coordination was critical. The Avisio viaduct was part of the famous Brenner Pass, which was the rail route across and over the Alps between Italy and Austria.

The remainder of the mission planning was my responsibility: routes, altitudes, takeoff times, speeds, bombing run direction, ordinance, escape and evasion, fighter escort rendezvous, and radio frequencies all had to be worked out. Plus, I had to brief the entire group in the morning.

I called my officers to the ops building and divided the workload among them. Frank was to plan the navigation, Charlie the bombing run and ordnance to be used, and Fred the intelligence, and I would pull it all together and prepare the mission briefing for the following day. I would get it approved by the ops officer. By this time in our tour, we were a well-honed team and our planning effort went smoothly. By midnight, we had the mission planned and I took it to Maj. Burtnett.

I gave him the written operational order and proceeded to brief him on it. He quickly perused the written order while I was talking and interrupted me with only this question, "Horn, you aren't going to run my airplanes out of fuel, are you?" I looked at him and snapped, "No, Sir!" He cracked a smile and said the plan looked fine and he would see me at the briefing in the morning.

Wake-up was at 0330 for a 0600 take off. Fred, Frank, Charlie, and I hustled to the mess hall. When I walked through the door, Harvey was there with the rest of the crew. He said, "Cap, in honor of you leading the group today, we have a presentation." I said, "Uh, OK, what is it?" Harvey ceremoniously unwrapped his handkerchief and inside were two real eggs! He took them over to Cookie who was standing at the griddle, and handed him the eggs. Cookie said, "How do you want 'em, sir?" I thought for a moment and said, "Just mix them with the powdered eggs, so we can all have a share." I was pretty touched at this simple gesture from my crew.

We wolfed down the chow and made for the briefing room just as most of the crews were drifting in to breakfast. Everything was set up by the time the crews came for the briefing around 0445. The whole thing went like clockwork, and I don't mind saying it made me proud.

The group commander, Lt.-Col. McGrath caught me on the way to our plane, Tailwind, and said, "Good job!" The opportunity to plan and lead a mission was a tremendous learning experience that gave me a new appreciation of the men in the unit who did it every day. A lot of them were not air crewmen, but enlisted men who were seldom recognized for their "desk" jobs. Our lives were in their hands daily and they never failed us.

The mission itself was kind of anticlimactic, after all the preparation. We had two aircraft turn back for maintenance issues. Frank's route kept us over water most of the time and his navigation was spot-on. We hit the IP for the bombing to the second and bombed at 20,000 feet. There was moderate accurate flak in the target area and we took several shards of shrapnel in Tailwind, as did the entire flight. All the aircraft made it home, though. BDA later assessed that we did a good job on the target. We arrived home at 1315 hours for a total of 07 + 15 of flight time for mission 48.

On August 30, we flew an ash-and-trash mission to Naples. I didn't need the gunners or bombardier, but they all wanted to go to the big PX in Naples, so we flew with a full crew. We had to pick up some specialized maintenance technicians and deliver them to San Pan to conduct training on the B-24Js. We flat-hatted it all the way to and from Naples, which was great fun after the high-altitude missions.

We were on the September 1 mission schedule to bomb a railroad bridge in Kraljevo, Yugoslavia. It was a short mission of only 04+45 hours flying time, directly northeast across the Adriatic from San Pan. There was no fighter escort and, thankfully, it was not needed. Flak was absent over the target and, overall, mission 49 was a milk run.

Our last mission, number 50, was scheduled for September 4. When the mission sheet came out before supper, I had a twinge in my gut. We needed one more and then we all could go back to the "world" and our loved ones. The war was going pretty much the way of the Allies in Europe and would be over soon. We had just one more trip.

I got the crew together after supper and we talked of finishing up this last mission as professionally as the first: heads in the game, no foul ups, and safety above all. The next day we discovered the mission was to bomb the Avisio railroad bridge again. We were to be the B box leader flying Little Jot, one of the newer B-24Js. The last time we were there, on August 27, significant and damaging flak was plentiful and most of the formation received some damage. There was nothing to be done about that except to pray that our luck held out. The crew double-checked the airplane after our meeting and Harvey reported that it was a fine ship.

Takeoff time was a bankerly 0930, which meant a few extra hours of sleep. The briefing went as normal and we had a fighter escort, although enemy fighters were not expected around the target area. The flight route was a replay of the previous trip. The lead navigator wasn't as sharp as Frank and he needed some prompting over the Adriatic. Everything was proceeding according to the plan. We encountered "scant, inaccurate flak" (Ulmer,

1944) in the target area, which was a welcome break after the last trip.

Frank lined us up for the bomb run. Charlie took control of the ship and a few minutes later barked, "Bomb bay doors open." Nothing happened. The notoriously finicky B-24 bomb bay doors had struck again. We recycled the switch and nothing happened.

The bombardier and I both had emergency releases we could use to open the doors and salvo the bombs. A quick conference between Charlie and me determined that I would employ this backup release mechanism. I gave the lever a mighty heave and the doors didn't open, but the bombs were released. We "dropped bombs through the doors" (Ulmer, 1944). It wasn't pretty, but we sent our last message to Hitler and the Axis.

Little Jot was wounded, with shredded bomb bay doors flapping in the wind stream and freezing air whipping through her innards: not a good situation for the box leader. After breaking left off the target, I radioed 2nd Lieut. H.V. Floerke and asked him to take over the lead because we could not keep up the formation speed. I descended out of the lead slot and he took over. We picked up the tail-end Charlie position as the group disappeared in front of us.

Frank had calculated that we could maintain 140 mph and have plenty of fuel to get home. As it turned out, because of the formation's navigational errors, we arrived at San Pan only 20 minutes behind them. We logged 07 + 15 for our 50th mission.

Our last mission was over and it was time to think about life again. We had flown 267 combat hours in 50 missions over a period of about four months. We had not lost anyone on the crew when we were together. I still had pangs of regret about Allen Bunker's death while serving with another crew. We all felt a sense of accomplishment and we shared a few drinks together that evening.

Knowing my combat flying was over for a while, "I could go to bed now and sleep." We all knew it would be a couple of months before we got home—that was the Army! While awaiting transport, I took leave and saw Rome, Naples, and a lot of country in between. The Italian people I met were destitute and war-weary, but very happy the Germans were gone and the U.S. Forces were occupying them.

When I entered the Army, I didn't know if I could make it: complete all the training successfully, go to war, and survive. My self-doubt was due to youth and a lack of experience. All wars are fought by 18 to 24-year-olds, and by that measure, I was among the older combatants. Once overseas, the self-doubt morphed into the nagging question, "How am I going to get out of this?"

In the end, my sense of duty absorbed during my upbringing, the ability to control my own fears and focus on the mission, and the technical competence the Army provided, gave me the answer to the question. War is a self-disclosing and defining experience for those who go. It was no different for me. After my wartime experience, I never doubted my ability again.

Finally, the saying, "There are no atheists in foxholes" is absolute truth. I was fortunate to have had a good Catholic upbringing, a supportive family, and a wonderful crew, and I was assigned to one of the most storied units in the Army Air Force. With the sage advice of Father Murphy and the benevolence of the good Lord, I learned how to give it up, how to trust, and how to ask for His help. He always came through.

I received orders to board a troop ship in Bari on October 10 for return passage. It was not exactly a first class ride, like the B-24 we flew overseas, but the destination was the most beautiful place in the world, the U.S.A. I arrived in Virginia on October 22, 1944. Boy, was I happy! The shipload of G.I.s was quickly processed and we were on trains destined for all over the United States. My train took me directly to New York City where I changed for the train to Albany, which stopped in Newburgh.

Every returning warrior dreams about coming home and his reunion with family and friends. Returning to Newburg and Eleanore and our families was extraordinary and never to be forgotten. Eleanore, Mom, Dad, Maggie, and even little Peter were all there on the platform to meet me. When Eleanore saw me, she ran and embraced me, duffel bag and all. I had missed her so much, more than I even admitted to myself. Now I was back in the embrace of my family. I thanked God for my deliverance and prayed that those still overseas would soon feel the joy that filled my heart.

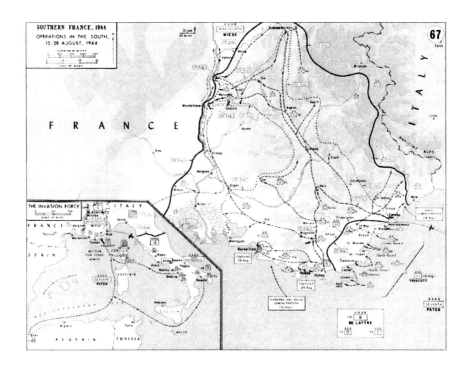

Map of Operation Dragoon.
Wikipedia via author.

Epilogue

AFTER my overseas tour, I was assigned to Bryan Army Airfield, later to become Bryan Air Force Base, near Bryan, Texas and Texas A&M University. I was there as an instructor pilot, flying the AT-6, until May of 1945, when I was sent to Buckingham Army Airfield in Fort Myers, Florida for demobilization. I was discharged from the Army on May 25, 1945. Eleanore and I enjoyed our time in the service, as brief as it was, but we were anxious to get on with our lives. Within three months, I had a job as a pilot for National Airlines, stationed in Jacksonville, Florida. Eleanore and I moved to Florida in August 1945, where we started our family.

I took no joy in the concept of war. It was a duty to defend the nation and an endurance contest of putting up with the poor living conditions and loneliness of being away from home. Aggressiveness—prosecuting violence and killing—was not something to be proud of under any guise and was not in my nature. I loved the flying part of it and would not have traded that for anything.

That the war was necessary was understood and everyone had a part to play. My combat experience was not something that I enjoyed talking about or reliving. The hours of boredom punctuated by moments of high anxiety, and intense fear and emotions were not things I wanted to recall. That isn't to say that once in a lifetime camaraderie, light moments, and wonderful travel experiences did not exist: they did.

The gut-wrenching experiences were what populated my memory and I could not relive that, so I didn't talk about it. As I grew older, another element played into my reluctance to speak about it. My thoughts centered on all those who didn't return. I guess it was delayed survivor's remorse. I had been living a wonderful life all these years after the war. They never had a chance.

This made me very sad and brought my emotions to just below the surface. I didn't trust myself to talk about it for fear of being overcome. There go I, but for the grace of God.

Being a part of the defining event of the 20th century was gratifying and an element of pride for me, but that was where my recollections ended. That the Army gave me an opportunity to go to war doing something I loved was a Divine gift. I tried to always keep that in mind and to be thankful in the way I lived my life.

I was one of millions in World War II who did their jobs. I was mighty lucky and blessed to have come home unscathed. Most of the real learning about air combat was on the job. Military schools and training don't really produce combat-ready men and women. They produce attitudes as well as thinking and re-acting skills. Actual combat is the real teacher. I am forever grateful to my crew and the leaders of the 376th who suffered my inexperience and naiveté. Without their patience, I would not have developed into a competent, safe, and living combat pilot.

Combat is defining. It is a once-in-a-lifetime chance to serve others—comrades, crew, family, and country—where the stakes are incalculable, a privilege only the youngest of our society can experience.

Air Route to Italy

- Departed Topeka, Kansas, 0600, 13 April 1944
- Arrived West Palm Beach, Florida, 1630
- Departed West Palm Beach, Florida, 0630, 15 April 1944
- Arrived Trinidad, 1630
- Departed Trinidad, 0500, 17 April 1944
- Arrived Belem, 1400
- Departed Belem, 0700, 18 April 1944
- Arrived Fontelza, 1020
- Departed Fontelza, 2400, 19 April 1944
- Arrived Dakkar, 1600
- Departed Dakkar, 0700, 2 May 1944
- Arrived Tinouf, Algeria, 1430
- Departed Tindouf, 0800, 3 May 1944
- Arrived Marrekesh, 1020
- Departed Marrakesh, 0730, 7 May 1944
- Arrived Tunis, 1400
- Departed Tunis 0600, 8 May 1944
- Arrived Giola, Italy, 1000
- Departed Giola, 13 May 1944
- Arrived San Pancrazio

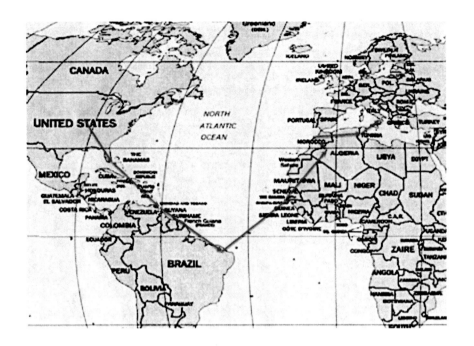

Air route to Italy.
Via author.

Appendix B

San Pancrazio Today

IN February–March 2015, I made a trip to San Pancrazio Salentino in the Province of Brindisi, state of Puglia, Italy, as part of the research for this book. In contrast to most of Europe, not much had changed in San Pancrazio in the 70 years since the 376th was there. It was still a sleepy farming community off the beaten path. The slow pace today makes it easy to imagine the astonishment the residents must have felt in 1943-1944, when first the Germans and then the Americans descended on them. However, that was not the first invasion of this area.

San Pancrazio has been an ancient Messapian settlement since the 8th century. The place has a healthy climate and a wonderful position on the Lecce plateau, not far from the Ionian coast. It was bestowed commune status when King Ferdinand II visited in1838. He was welcomed by a little girl bearing wildflowers, which she had just picked in his honor. The sovereign was so taken by the gesture that he gave commune status to the place.

The most noteworthy event in the history of the town, before the Americans arrived, was a Turkish raid in 1547. Five Turkish vessels landed at Torre Colimena, south of San Pancrazio, on the night of January 1. The invaders were guided by a traitor named Chiara, who led them to the town. The Turks rounded up all the inhabitants and took them to Turkey, where they were sold as slaves. The town was refounded and populated with new inhabitants several years later under the leadership of Francesco Aleandro, who established a summer residence there for the bishops of Brindisi.

San Pancrazio remains a vibrant farming community, where the temperate climate facilitates the growth of ancient olive trees, grain, cut flowers, and the diminutive but flavorful Negroamaro grape used to make the unique wines of Puglia. You need to try them!

After spending a few days in "San Pan," I could see how the servicemen stationed here in World War II enjoyed the place. The pace was slow, the people kind and open to strangers, and the seafood excellent. And the wine? Well, I covered that above.

I stayed in the Agriturisimo Torrevecchi B&B owned by three brothers. The B&B was clearly a sideline to their farming, cut flowers, lamb, and winery businesses. Torrevecchi was operated by a petite young woman, Chiara, the daughter of one of the brothers. Chiara was a law student in at Universita del Salento, Lecce. She spoke English perfectly and was a fabulous host. The oversized rooms and the excellent restaurant were in an old stone building with Roman arches and covered patios overlooking a modern pool.

On the B&B property was the archeological site of the small church of Santo Antonio, with a crypt excavated in the rock that contained frescos telling the terrible story of the sack of the town by the Turks.

My purpose in travelling to San Pan was to interview a few people who might have some memories of the Americans stationed there during World War II and to see the airfield, which I knew still existed from Google Earth photos.

The airfield was originally built by the Germans. It was improved dramatically and used by the Americans. It is one of the few 15th Air Force bases in Puglia that stands almost untouched. It is no longer used as an airfield and is fenced off behind threatening security signs. The weeds are coming thru the cracks in the hardstand and the soft surface taxiways have been reclaimed by nature.

The stone farmhouse requisitioned from the Scarpelli family was still there, as were several other buildings identified in old photographs. There were no sentries; I was able to go through a hole in the fence and stand on the runway where my father flew into combat in 1944. It was a very personal and powerful connection for me with my Dad.

A few residents still had memory of when the American air armada descended on the countryside in 1943-1944, and I found two of them: Signorina Pasqualini Scarpelli and Signorina Maria

Giringelli. My interviews with them are in Appendices B and C, respectively. They remembered the Americans as warm and generous occupiers who created the most excitement in San Pancrazio in their lifetimes.

San Pan will continue to go its quiet way, anonymously provisioning Italy and the world through its vibrant agriculture, until the next invaders appear.

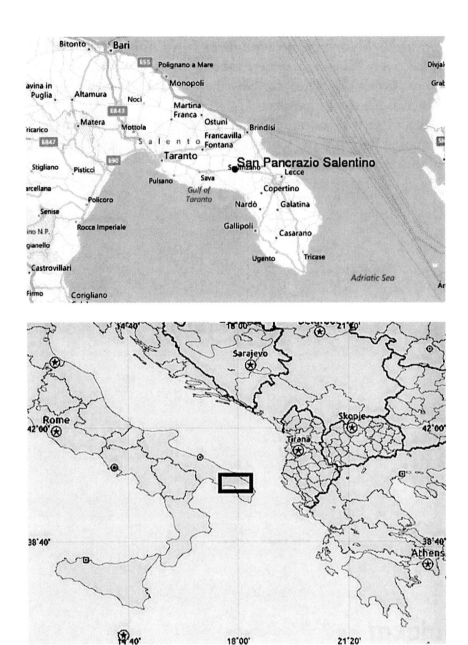

Maps showing location of San Panzrazio, Italy.

San Pancrazio airfield, 2015.
Author photo.

Appendix C

Author's Interview with Pasqualina Scarpello, March 1, 2015, San Pancrazio, Italy

I was born in San Pancrazio in 1929. We did not see much of the war's violence in our town because we had nothing of military value. There was never any fighting in our area. The Germans came in 1940 or 1941 and built a small airfield* and base near my grandparents' farmhouse northeast of town. They kept to themselves and we saw very little of them. Occasionally a convoy of German vehicles might come through town. Sometimes they stopped at the city hall to meet with the town council.

After the invasion of Sicily, the Germans disappeared from our area. Shortly thereafter, the Americans came. The Germans isolated themselves. They didn't steal from us, even though they were poorly provisioned. When the Germans retreated, they destroyed everything that could not be taken with them. They also mounted a propaganda campaign to convince us that the coming Americans were evil.

When the Americans arrived, they occupied the same area as the Germans had, but expanded the base and airfield greatly. My grandparents' farmhouse was needed for the larger base and they had to move. I don't remember any bad feelings about this, but I was young. We were still able to farm our land around the base, so that was something.

I had no interactions with American GIs other than seeing them around town, and I never heard of any problems in San Pancrazio. GIs always had a procession of children behind them because they had candy and chocolate. They were very kind and the children considered them like Father Christmas, even better than Father Christmas, because of the treats they had.

Before the war, there was no chocolate in San Pancrazio. It seems a strange thing that Americans introduced it to us. It goes to show how small and undeveloped San Pancrazio was in those days. Another thing I remember was the Black soldiers. I had never seen a Black person before the Americans arrived.

All the American men at the base seemed so old to me at the time, but they were only a half dozen years older than I was. The GIs did fraternize with the local girls and I know of one who married an American and moved to the United States. There were a few Italian-American babies left behind in San Pancrazio, too. Fair hair was the indication: we accepted that the child had American parentage. This was silly, of course, because there were many soldiers with olive complexions, just like the Italians.

The war caused us to suffer many deprivations. We were farmers and could raise enough to feed ourselves, but it was impossible to get manufactured goods. There was no sugar or salt or condiments of any kind. Of all the difficulties I remember, the lack of shoes was the worst. The Americans came through for us though and gave us shoes.

Technology did not exist in Puglia until the Americans came. We went from a preindustrial farm community to a hi-tech aviation community in a few months. The Americans created a lot of jobs, but I didn't know anyone who worked for them. All of my family and extended family worked the land.

There were no airplanes in San Pancrazio before the war. The Germans built the airfield when they came, but the Americans improved and extended it. The noise and activity of the airfield didn't bother me normally, but if I was working in the fields around the base, it could be disturbing because they were so close. I had no idea of what all those great airplanes were doing every day.

When the Americans left in the summer of 1945, they left everything behind that was not transportable. Cottage industries sprang up in San Pancrazio, salvaging the remnants of the base. My family's farmhouse was returned and inside it had been painted and repaired. I remember my grandfather saying that the Americans were the best tenants he ever had and he wanted them to come back and work on the outside of the house!

One other thing I remember is that the Americans requisitioned the house of my son-in-law Giovanni's family located in the town. They moved all the family furniture into one room to make room for their office furniture. Giovanni's family's furniture was badly damaged in the process of storage. I don't know if they were ever compensated for that.

The war years were exciting for me, as I look back. I don't remember the material hardships so clearly now. San Pancrazio, luckily, was untouched by fighting. The Germans were absentee occupiers and committed none of the mischief and criminality we heard about in other parts of Italy. The Americans were friendly and generous "house guests" that introduced San Pancrazio to 20th-century technology. Our town has reverted to a sleepy farming community today, but that does not diminish the pride of those of us who remember hosting the Americans during the war.

Authors Note: The fact that the Germans built the airfield is new information. All of the sources I found indicated the airfield was built by the Americans in 1943. The physical layout of the airfield as it exists today supports the theory that it was built in two phases and for different types of aircraft. From the Google Earth photo and my own ground observations, it was easy to see two distinctly different surfaces on the runway: one was a longer light-colored, hard-packed rock surface, still intact. The northernmost part of the runway was a dark-colored surface, almost like macadam. It was significantly overgrown and was probably the original German airfield, used for much lighter aircraft than the B-24.

Pasqualina Scarpello.
Author photo.

Crashed B-24 at San Pancrazio with Scarpello farmhouse in background.
Via author.

Appendix D

Author's Interview with Maria Giringelli, March 1, 2015, San Panacrazio, Italy

I was born in 1930 and was a teenager during the war years. My family lived in San Pancrazio, which was a peaceful agricultural village in Puglia of no strategic value. We were bypassed by most of the violence in the war. There was a partisan group that operated from our town, but being a teenage girl, I was excluded from any detailed knowledge of the resistance. Puglia [in English, Apulia] was one of the poorer and less developed regions of Italy. During the war, living and working was difficult. We only had what we could grow ourselves.

During the time the asino [jackass] Mussolini was still complicit with Hitler and Italy was a member of the AXIS, we generally had enough to eat and work was plentiful. When Italy surrendered to the Allies in September 1943, the Germans around San Pancrazio simply disappeared and moved north.

They were not lawless occupiers, although they seldom gave us a fair price for the goods they took. They kept pretty much to themselves on their own bases. We were warned by the Germans and the remaining fascists that the Americans were coming and that they were evil. The partisans told us we could expect better treatment from the American forces, based on the experience in Sicily, and that gave us some hope.

There are a few memories that stand out in my mind from during those years. I had been sent on an errand by my father to another village a few kilometers away. On the return journey, I was walking on a road between open fields when I heard an airplane and saw it as a distant dot in the sky. It got louder and louder and gave the impression it was coming straight for me. Being buzzed or machine gunned from the air was not unheard of, so I didn't think it strange or question why I should be singled out. As I dove into the ditch on the side of the road, the plane seemed to fly inches above my head, its engine screaming, but with no guns firing. It went straight on and crashed within seconds, perhaps a hundred yards beyond me. I was frightened and didn't even bother to go and look at it, but carried on home as fast as I could.

Another incident that I heard about from my uncle, who lived in Foggia, was that two drunken German soldiers forced their way into his house when he was about to go to bed, and said to him: "We've occupied France, Belgium, Holland, and Poland, and tonight we are going to occupy your wife." My uncle brazenly replied, "You can occupy the whole world, but not my wife. I'm a bachelor." In their disappointment, the Germans smashed all his furniture and destroyed whatever else they could before leaving.

I used to lie on my straw mattress at night wondering. "Will I survive the war?" One day I really thought that my luck had run out. I was in the courtyard of our house when a member of the Brigate Nere [a Fascist paramilitary group] came in carrying a submachine gun. He was 16; he actually told me his age. I knew that these young thugs were inexperienced and apt to panic and fire off at the least excuse or just to show off.

He asked me who lived there and I told him it was our house. Suddenly I remembered that "Long Live Badoglio!" [Marshal Pietro Badoglio, Italian head of government who signed the armistice between Italy and the Allies on September 3, 1943] was painted on the white wall to the side of our door and I thought he might find it. It was covered by brushwood bundles, but still? Supporting any opposition to the remaining Fascists was a death sentence if you were caught. The young thug had just started to talk to me, boasting about his age and showing me his dagger and gun, when someone from his group called his name and he left. I felt a huge sigh of relief.

In early 1943, the Germans planned a rastrellamento [search and round-up] in San Pancrazio. Men from 14 to 50 were rounded up and sent to work in Germany or other places. My father was caught up in this and sent to Austria. This was my lowest point. Without my father to guide the family, I didn't really believe we would survive the war. He was gone for almost a year, but following the armistice, he was able to return home.

The American Air Force arrived en masse all over Puglia in the fall of 1943. They were building dozens of airfields from which to fly their airplanes. Labor was in demand. In contrast to German occupation practices, the Americans did not impress labor, but recruited and paid the Italians fairly to help in the construction efforts. The scale of the projects was beyond anything we could imagine. This was our first introduction to technology. It seems difficult to believe today and there is very little physical evidence of it, other than the dilapidated old airfield near town.

The Americans we came in contact with or heard about were civilized occupiers. They did not harass us, steal, or attack the villagers. With the American operations in San Pancrazio, there were jobs, many for women. My mother got a job as a housekeeper and laundry woman around Christmas 1943. She worked for four officers, washing their clothes, polishing their shoes, and keeping their tented living area clean. Those four officers did their job and were sent home and others took their place in the tent. My mother's services were just passed along to the new officers. I have no recollection of any of their names.

It was because of their generosity that we did not starve. Now that my mother had a job, we could afford to buy food, but there was none to buy. The Americans were deeply involved in fighting the Germans and could not feed themselves and the population too. The men my mother worked for provided for us, giving her leftovers from where they ate, and food and candy from packages and cans. It was very foreign food to us, but we were lucky to have it. It was not uncommon in the last years of the war for people to die of malnutrition in San Pancrazio. The Americans even gave her candy and treats to give to me.

The air over Puglia was alive each day with the roaring of the huge bombers going and coming. I could not imagine these huge machines dropping tons of explosives, every day, in places thousands of miles away. All night, rain or shine, the base was full of the activities necessary to make the planes ready for the next day's mission. Sometimes during the day, when the airplanes were gone, young American soldiers would walk to the village to buy souvenirs or wine or to see the ladies.

We were only too happy to trade with these young men. Some people even cheated them, but those were harsh times and Italians did things to stay alive that they wouldn't do in normal times. We had nothing and it was hard to be critical of those struggling to live. Many of the men had cameras and took a lot of pictures. One day, a few of these men saw me and asked me to pose with them for a picture. Although only 14 at the time, I was quite grown up physically, and this was apparently the side of me they wanted to photograph. I was posing with the men and acting the diva. It was all quite innocent, but I often wondered who saw the photos and what stories were told about them.

We could not get salt, or any other manufactured or processed goods. No salt was an agony for us. At first, rock salt for the animals was consumed, and then empty barrels of salted fish were either soaked or scraped. Finally, there was none at all. People suffered from recurring headaches. Normally, even if you do not sprinkle salt on your food, there is plenty of it as a preservative, but we had no processed food. The entire area was completely and totally without salt.

To add to the misery, the winter of 1944 was the coldest ever. The temperature in Puglia fell to an unprecedented minus 6 degrees centigrade. All the fuel had been stolen or used up and we had no heat. It was the worst winter of my life. The fountain tap in the square, our only source of water, froze. In spite of the continuing wretchedness and deprivation, when the Americans arrived, I felt that we would survive the war.

The Americans began leaving San Pancrazio in the summer of 1945 and were gone by the fall. The aerodrome is still there on the northwest of the town. It has seen only a little use in the last 70 years. San Pancrazio quickly reverted back to a sleepy Italian village, but it took many years for the prosperous agricultural activities to recover from the war damage. Even though there was no fighting in our area, the war destroyed thousands of fruit and olive trees. Vineyards where the black negroamaro grape made famous by this region grows had been ravaged and spoiled by the war. Puglia did not receive much reconstruction help, either from the Allies or from the multitude of Italian governments we endured after the war.

I have lived here all my life and can say that the German withdrawal and the American arrival was the most exciting time of my life. The level of the American effort in San Pancrazio to end the war, multiplied all over Europe, seemed to us an irresistible force that would make it possible for normal times to return. The arrival of the Americans gave us hope.

I hope this gives you some information about what San Pancrazio was like during the war and what your father might have seen.

Maria Giringelli.
Author photo.

Distinguished Flying Cross Award

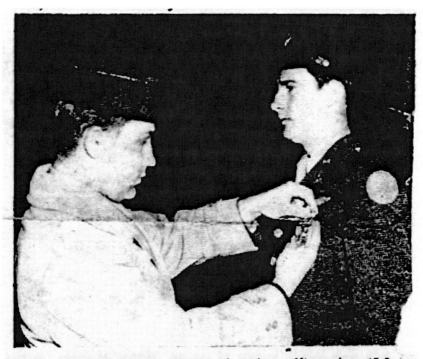

LIEUT. JOHN H. HORN, member of student officer class 45-2, re-
ceives the Distinguished Flying Cross from Lt/Col. Christian B. Walk
who made the presentation on behalf of Maj/Gen. Nathan Twining,
Commanding General 15th Air Force. The award was made for extraordinary achievement in connection with the bombing of Marsielle
harbor prior to the invasion of southern France.

Distinguished Flying Cross awarded to Lt. John H. Horn.
Newburgh Free Press via author.

Works Consulted

376th Heavy Bombardment Group. Retrieved from 376th Bomb Group Veterans Association website, 2013.

Ambrose, S. *The Wild Blue*. New York, NY: Touchstone, 2002.

Barron, J. "John Kane, 89, who led raid that bombed Nazi's oil depot." (Obituary). June 12, 1996. Retrieved from The New York Times website.

BBC. "On this Day: June 5 (1944)." London, England. Retrieved from BBC website.

Bonn, K. *When the Odds Were Even: The Vosges Mountain Campaign, October 1944-January 1945*. New York, NY: Ballantine, 2006.

Capps, R. *Flying Colt*. Bloomington, IN: Author House, 2004.

Clendenin, E. *376th Bomb Group Mission History* (3rd ed.). Colleyville, TX: Clendenin, 2010.

Consolidated Aircraft, Flight and Service Department. *Flight Manual B-24D Airplane*. San Diego, CA: Consolidated Aircraft Corporation, 1942.

Currier, D. R. *Fifty Mission Crush*. Shippensburg, PA: Burd Street Press, 1992.

Horn, J. E. Interview with Maria Ghringelli. San Pancrazio, Italy. Personal contact, 2015.

—. Interview with Pasqualina Scarpello. San Pancrazio, Italy. Personal contact, 2015.

—. Personal recollections. Personal contact, 1946-2002.

Horn, J. H. Master Pilot Log. San Pancrazio, Italy: Unpublished, 1944.

Horn, L. Interview with John H. Horn. Sebastion, FL: Unpublished, 1999.

Katz, R. *The Battle for Rome: The Germans, the Allies, the Partisans, and the Pope, September 1943–June 1944*. New York, NY: Simon & Schuster, 2003.

Klar, L. Silent Sleep. 1944. Retrieved from the 330th Bomb Group (VH) page on the Ancestry website.

Mark, J. J. *Battle of Cannae*. Retrieved from the Ancient History Encyclopedia web site, 2011.

McManus, J. *Deadly Sky*. Novato, CA: Presido Press, 2000.

Sonder, F., Jr. "Preparing Our Flyers for Combat." Condensed from *American Legion Magazine*, Readers Digest, 42 (250), February 1943.

Stritof, S. "Estimated Median Age at First Marriage, by Sex: 1890 to 2012." 2014. Retrieved from About Relationships website.

Tillman, B. *Forgotten Fifteenth*. Washington DC: Regnery, 2014.

Ulmer, H. H. "Mission Diary." San Pancrazio, Italy: Unpublished, 1944.

Yerian, D. E. *Bombs Over Europe: Stories of a B-24 Bomber Group From the Famed "Liberandos" and Their Missions Over Occupied Europe During 1944*. Raleigh, NC: Lulu Press, Inc., 2008.

CPSIA information can be obtained
at www.ICGtesting.com
Printed in the USA
LVOW07s1254140517
534488LV00007B/547/P